T0365250

authorHouse Books by Dr. Deborah Manoushka Paul Figaro

Understanding Dreams, Visions, and
Prophecies, A Bible-Based Approach...
Comprendre Les Rêves Les Visions, Et Les
Prophéties, Une Approche Biblique...

A PLAN,
a PRESENTATION and
a DRAFT
of
An ANALYSIS on the
US ECONOMIC SANCTIONS
& the CUBAN EMBARGO

Dr. Deborah Manoushka Paul Figaro

authorHOUSE·

AuthorHouse™
1663 Liberty Drive
Bloomington, IN 47403
www.authorhouse.com
Phone: 833-262-8899

Published by AuthorHouse 03/18/2021

ISBN: 978-1-6655-1909-0 (sc)
ISBN: 978-1-6655-1926-7 (e)

Print information available on the last page.

Any people depicted in stock imagery provided by Getty Images are models, and such images are being used for illustrative purposes only.
Certain stock imagery © Getty Images.

This book is printed on acid-free paper.

Because of the dynamic nature of the Internet, any web addresses or links contained in this book may have changed since publication and may no longer be valid. The views expressed in this work are solely those of the author and do not necessarily reflect the views of the publisher, and the publisher hereby disclaims any responsibility for them.

I dedicate this book to my professors
at
St Thomas University, School of Law

Dr. iur. Siegfried Wiessner and Professor Dr. Roza Pati

INTRODUCTION

The ANALYSIS on the US ECONOMIC SANCTIONS & the CUBAN EMBARGO is an Analysis I presented live in a seminar at St Thomas University, School of Law when I was asked to locate and identify a human rights problem or violation, to analyze it, addressing discrete and sensitive issues in the field, discussing the idea of hegemonic human rights laws, and then to find resolutions to the problem using The New Haven School of Jurisprudence, which is a school of thought that "offers a framework of interdisciplinary analysis of societal problems and a heuristic for inventing policy alternatives and recommending solutions that apply across cultures, throughout the planet, and over time."

The New Haven School of Jurisprudence is a policy-oriented perspective on international law from which its intellectual antecedents lie in sociological jurisprudence of Roscoe Pound and the reformist ambitions of the American Legal Realists. Nathan Roscoe Pound was an American legal scholar and educator who served as Dean of Havard Law School from 1916 to 1936, a member of the faculty of UCLA School of Law in the school early years, from 1949 to 1952, and identified as one of the most cited legal scholars of the 20th century by The Journal of Legal Studies.

From the perspective of the New Haven School of Jurisprudence approach, jurisprudence is a theory about making social choices, where its primary jurisprudential and intellectual tasks are the prescription and application of policy in ways that maintain community order and simultaneously achieve the best possible approximation of the community's social goals, which include maximizing shared community values, such as wealth, well-being, enlightenment, skill, affection, respect, morality, integrity and rectitude, having for goal the interpretation of international law as a system of creating minimum world public order, with continued progress toward the development of shared values into the most advantageous order.

Thus, I located and identified some human rights violations in the midst of the US economic sanctions and the Cuban embargo. In this book, using The New Haven School of Jurisprudence, I analyzed the problem, I addressed the issues, discussed the idea of hegemonic human rights laws, and then recommended solutions that should apply across and throughout both countries, and over time.

PART I

THE PLAN
on
An analysis on
The Economic Sanctions
& the Cuban Embargo

A- Introduction:

The purpose of this analysis is to find a solution for the U.S.-Cuba 'awkward' relationship regarding the ongoing sanctions the US put on Cuba decades ago when Fidel Castro, the Cuban leader, refused to abide by the American democratic system, decided instead to have his country under the communist system. Many thinkers have tried to come up with solutions for the two countries, but their relationship has remained just about the same for over 53 years now. Today American authorities are trying to change things and want to release the sanctions.

The key questions are, is it a good idea? What would be the outcome? And then, why? Why now? This analysis will answer those questions by starting to give a brief historical background of Cuban politic; next, it will use a five step process that one should make that the New Haven School recommends when solving problems. The process consists of the delimitation of the problem, the identification of the conflicting claims, the test of past decisions and its conditioning factors, the projection of future decisions, and the appraisal of past and future decisions including the recommendations. Last, this analysis will conclude with my personal thoughts.

B- Brief Historical background of Cuban politics

   a. Before Castro
       – Free country (Barbudos [bearded revolutionaries] and Ernesto 'Che' Guevara)
       – 'Libertinage': had in and out Americans, another Las Vegas, mafia (movies: Scarface)
       – Ernest Heminguay, American writer author of the Kilimanjaro

b. Brief history of US/Castro relationships

c. Castro's period – How is or was the system under Castro?-Capitalism turned into communism.

d. Present

C- The five problem-solving steps recommended by the New Haven School

I- Observation, Clarification, and Delimitation of the problem

The problem – Ongoing US Economic sanctions on Cuba and restrictions on Cuban travel and commerce for all people and companies under the United State jurisdiction for decades – although it can be favorable, but it can be exceedingly deteriorating as well – an embargo that effectively barred even food and medicine.

Cause and effects of the embargo on Cuba caused by the US

a. Negative aspects of the embargo:
   i. exchange of the market being closed, they were not able to travel and expand; (The Black Book)

   ii. Cubans in Cuba, not in extreme poverty, but have not been able to eat properly; (The Black Book)

iii.   Cubans in Cuba have been involuntarily dispersed from their family – led to boat people;

iv.   Prostitution rate in Cuba used to be 0% until the economy collapsed caused by the embargo, which forced young women and men into prostitution. An author says it's an anomaly in Cuba; (James C. McKinley Jr. in The New York Times)

v.   Cuban economy collapsed partly because of the embargo [and partly when USSR that was assisting Cuba financially collapsed itself, Cuba's economy declined.] New York Times

b. Positive aspects of the embargo:

i.   Despite the embargo, Cuba managed to better the inhabitants education; literacy rate very high; became highly educated; Cubans are in all over the other part of the world; best doctors in Cuba; Cubans end up being the most humanitarian people in the world, helping and curing people everywhere even in Haiti; (Caribbean News)

ii.   despite the embargo, Cuba managed to keep its economy afloat with aid he's getting from the USSR; and when the USSR's economy collapsed, Cuba made a sudden change in the way of handling business; he allowed foreign investments and limited tourism in the country; (New York Times)

iii. The Cuban people might be struggling with other problems, but there is no homeless in Cuba, the system doesn't allow it to happen;

iv. Cuba is very catholic, stays in very close contact with Rome; they strictly go by what the Bible say, therefore, no dui, very low crime rate; strict or very disciplined;

v. Tourism: Canadians, Haitians, Mexicans, many people from other counties are regularly visiting Cuba. Exportation of the Cuban music is very wide within the Spanish world of America... CDs made in Canada, while the US refused to deal with them. Also, when Castro saw the economy was declining, he allowed foreign investments and limited tourism in the country; (New York Times)

vi. Despite the embargo in Cuba: they used the embargo time to better their education – the population is highly educated; a large number of people have graduate degrees – most likely have a good school system, because many people from many different developed countries go to Cuba for their higher education. According to UNESCO, their literacy rate is effectively 100%;

    vii.   Embargo was supposed to have a negative effect, but Castro turned it into positive;

    viii.   Managed to fix old American cars and resell to America;

    ix.   Became number one sellers of cigars, best cigars in the world (tobacco);

c.   <u>Just to compare</u>-Brief comparison between embargo in Haiti when they had an about 3 years of embargo, didn't know what to do and how to handle it, it totally devastated the whole country.

II- Identification, Classification, of Conflicting Claims

a.   <u>Who are the claimants and what do they claim</u>?

    i.   The United States – They want to release the sanctions.

    ii.   The Allied and the proponents (some agree, some don't)

b.   <u>Advocate institutions</u>

      i.   UN: The General Assembly adopted a resolution calling for an end to the economic, commercial, and financial blockade imposed by the United States against Cuba. http://www.ohchr.org/EN/countries/LACRegion/Pages/CUIndex.aspx

      ii.   Other organizations?
Within the 193-nation assembly, 188 countries elected for the nonbinding resolution, titled "Necessity of Ending the Economic, Commercial and Financial Embargo imposed by the United States of America against Cuba." http://www.ohchr.org/EN/countries/LACRegion/Pages/CUIndex.aspx

c. The claimants' perspectives (what did they want decades ago – now what/why?)

      i.   The United States wanted for decades for Cuba to become Democratic or to preoccupy Cuba, they sanctioned the Cuba for non collaborating – now WHY do they want to release the sanctions?

      ii.   The UN condemned Cuba for 'Human Rights violations' – Now they are being controversial. They condemn the decades-long U.S. economic embargo against Cuba. Why?

iii. Proponents of the embargo dispute that Cuba has not met what the US conditioned for lifting the embargo, which is the transitioning into democracy and the improvisation of human rights. New York Times.

iv. Other proponents think that the US should not be backing down because it will make the United States appear weak, and that simply the Cuban elite will benefit from the release of the embargo. New York Times.

v. On the other side, opponents of the embargo think that the embargo should be lifted because the US policy has failed has clearly not achieved its goals; they think that the sanctions have instead harmed the US economy and Cuban citizens, and prevented opportunities to promote changes and democracy in Cuba, and that instead, the embargo has hurt international opinion of the United States. New York Times.

d. The claimants' bases of power

III- Past trends in Decision and Conditioning Factors

a. How the world responded to these conflicting claims in the past

1. In 1964, the State Department Policy Planning Council states that the primary danger the US faces in Castro is that Castro represents a successful defiance of the US.

2. A writer, Thomas Paterson writes that Cuba, as symbol and reality, challenged US authority in Latin America.

3. In 1995, President Clinton signed an executive order to lift some travel restrictions and to allow a Western Union office to open in Havana. President Clinton said that "the embargo was a foolish, pandering failure..." because It allowed Castro to demonize the United States for decades...' He added that 'with half a brain' could see the embargo was counterproductive." US Magazine.

4. On the other hand, the George W. Bush administration added new, more severe restrictions to the embargo and increased penalties on Cuba.

5. Former Secretary of State Hillary Clinton alleged that the Castro regime has harmed US attempts to improve relations between them. Clinton believed that Castro does not want to end the embargo and normalize with the United States.

6. In 2004, President Obama (senator at that time) stated that "The Cuban embargo has failed to provide the sorts of rising standards of living, and has squeezed the innocents in Cuba and utterly failed to overthrow Castro, who has now been there since I was born. It is now time to acknowledge that that particular policy has failed." US News and the World Report.

7. In 2011, President Obama made steps to ease the Cuban embargo by lifting restrictions on travel and allowing transfers of funds, and also by asking to release political prisoners and to provide people with their basic human rights. US News and the World Report.

8. In 2011, US Ambassador to the UN Ronald Godard defended the sanctions as a means to support respect for human rights and basic freedoms. Godard claimed that the United States was helping the people of Cuba by sending funds in family remittances and in agricultural, medical, and humanitarian products.

The 'warfare' against Cuba has been very strongly condemned in virtually every relevant international forum. The European Union condemned the embargo. The Judicial Commission of the normally compliant Organization of American States has declared them illegal.

In the midst of all that, in 2012, Fidel Castro, in his late 80s, has been reportedly very ill and his younger brother Raúl Castro is also over 80 years old. Raúl was re-elected in Feb. 2013, at which time he announced that he would step down in 2018.

Some people hoped that a new regime would make the reforms necessary to annul the blockade, while others looked for President Obama to end the embargo regardless of Cuba's actions.

b. How did the US perform? Why did they fail?
   i. A close analysis of predispositional and environmental conditioning factors and how these factors influenced the operation (strategic interventions)

US attacks plots did not occur – too 'terrostic' – and US invasions were unsuccessful –

1. 1961-Bay of Pigs Invasion – A failed military invasion of Cuba undertaken by the CIA-sponsored paramilitary group, a Cuban exiles group.

2. 1962 – Operation Northwoods (Plot to blow up a US ship in Guantanamo Bay and blame Cuba and have a US military intervention in Cuba).

3. 1962 – Operation Mongoose ("Possible Actions to Provoke, Harass or Disrupt Cuba." It was a plan to create incident which would have the appearance of an attack on US facilities in Cuba, which would provide an excuse for the US military to invade and overthrow Castro.)

4. 1962 – Operation Dirty Trick (A plot to blame Castro)

5. 1962 – A plot to make it appear that Cuba had attacked a member of the Organization of American States (OAS)

6. A plot to bribe one of Castro's subordinate commanders to initiate an attack on the US Navy base at Guantanamo.

7. Body of Secrets

8. 1963 – Pretext – A plan to create a war between Cuba and another Latin American country so that the US would intervene.

9. 1964 – 'Destruction Operations" – President Kennedy approved the CIA plan to attack a large oil refinery and storage facilities... A plan to kill Castro.

10. 1969 – President Nixon's directed the CIA to intensify covert operations against Cuba.

11. 1970 – Under Nixon's government – A plot to attack fishing boats, embassies and Cuban offices overseas, and the bombing of a Cuban airliner killing all 73 passengers.

12. 1997-Bombings in Cuba

c. Legislative and Public Policy Framework

1. In 2012, Cuban Foreign Minister Bruno Rodriguez points out

to the UN General Assembly about "the inhumane, failed and anachronistic policy of 11 successive US administrations."

2. In 2013, the U N passed a resolution condemning the embargo for the 22nd consecutive year. The vote was 188/2, only Israel supported the US policy. US News & World Report

3. President Obama's new policy suggests the overall U.S. embargo on trade with Cuba remains in place and can only be lifted by Congressional action — "a step we strongly favor," President Obama says.

d. Laws

IV- Projection or Prediction of future trends

a. What the US seems to be going to decide
1. On Dec. 17, 2014, for the first time in the history, President Obama declared a re-establishment of full diplomatic relations with Cuba. In addition, while the US embargo remains in effect and ordinary tourism by Americans is still prohibited, the United States is

taking a step to ease travel and remittance restrictions, release three Cuban spies, and open an embassy in Havana.

2. Cuba on its side, agreed to release 53 Cubans identified by the United States as political prisoners, as well as an American and an unnamed intelligence agent who had been imprisoned for nearly 20 years.

3. However, a US Senator, Marco Rubio opposed the move, saying, "This is going to do absolutely nothing to further human rights and democracy in Cuba.

4. On May 29, 2015, the United States formally removed from Cuba the list of state sponsors of terrorism.

5. On July 1, 2015, President Obama announced in a speech at the White House: he has agreed to formally reestablish diplomatic relations with the Republic of Cuba and reopen embassies in our respective countries.

DR. DEBORAH MANOUSHKA PAUL FIGARO

6. As a sign of renewed diplomatic relations, the Cuban flag was raised over the country's Washington, DC, embassy on July 20, 2015 for the first time since diplomatic relations were cut off 54 years prior.

7. US Secretary of State John Kerry traveled to Cuba to hoist the American flag over the US embassy there on Aug. 14, 2015.

b. What could be the reason(s) or motive(s) – why? why now? – unclear reasons

1. Could be: Since the US tried to intervene so many times, never worked, now they want to do the opposite.

2. Could be: The US may want to apply the system "Je t'embrasse pour mieux t'ettouffer" – Sun Tzu, in The Art of War.

3. Could be: Cuba has the best doctors, and best at other things-let's all get along and share –

4. Could be: Releasing the embargo will benefit, culturally, economically...

5. A White House official said, the reestablishment of diplomatic relationship is being done because they believe that the policy of the past has not worked and that they believe the best way to bring democracy and prosperity to Cuba is through a different kind of policy."

V- Alternatives and Recommendations in the Global Common Interest

1. Evaluation of the release of the embargo and recommendations
    a. In order to attain goal of maximizing access by all to all the values humans desire, no more intervention.

Conclusion: (Personal input)

PART II

THE PRESENTATION
on
An analysis on
The Economic Sanctions
& the Cuban Embargo

- **The purpose** of this presentation is to find a solution for the U.S.-Cuba 'awkward' relationship regarding the ongoing sanctions the US put on Cuba decades ago when Fidel Castro, the Cuban leader, refused to abide by the American democratic system, decided instead to have his country under the communist system.

- Many thinkers have tried to come up with solutions for the two countries, but their relationship has remained just about the same for over 53 years now.

- Today American authorities are trying to change things and want to release the sanctions.

- The key questions are, is it a good idea? What would be the outcome? And then, why? Why now?

- This analysis will use the five step process of the New Haven School in order to find an answer to those questions. It will start first with a brief historical background of Cuban politics, and then will conclude with some personal thoughts.

A- A Brief Historical background of Cuban politics –

- **Before Castro**, Cuba used to be seen as "the brothel of the Western hemisphere" — an island inhabited by people whose main occupation was to cater to American tourists at Havana's luxurious hotels, beaches and casinos.

- Cuba was one of the **most advanced and successful** countries in Latin America.

- **Cuba's capital**, Havana, was a glittering and dynamic city.

- There was a '**libertinage**', it was like a free country, people were doing whatever they wanted as far as prostitution, drinking, and crimes.

- Americans were going in and out, it was another **Las Vegas**, with the drinking, gambling, mostly by the Americans.

- Then there were **the mafia**. In the movie Scarface, they talk about it, they show that tones of cocaine were coming to Cuba from Colombia through Miami...

- **And then**, there were profound **inequalities** in Cuban society – between the city and the countryside and between whites and blacks. In the countryside, some Cubans lived in terrible poverty.

- There were an army of **unemployed** people, perpetually in debt and living on the margins of survival.

- Many poor peasants were seriously **malnourished** and hungry.

- Neither **health care** nor **education** reached those countryside Cubans.

- **Illiteracy** was widespread, and those lucky enough to attend school rarely made it past the first or second grades.

- **Clusters of graveyards dotted the main highways**, marking the spots where people died waiting for transportation to the nearest hospitals and clinics.

- **Racism** also destroyed Cuban society.

- The island's private clubs and beaches were **segregated**.

- Even **President** <u>Fulgencio **Batista**</u>, **a mulatto**, was **denied membership** in one of Havana's most exclusive clubs.

- Cuba's social problems were compounded by a violent, chaotic and **corrupt political history**.

- **Since** their independence, **Cuba always had bad government**.

- It was a bloody and costly **struggle to achieve independence** from Spain, but all the good leaders were being killed.

- **Cuba was a democratic** country for about 12 years, with free elections, **but** it was a democracy spoiled by corruption and political violence –

- There were action groups or **gangs** who shot their way through politics.

- Some people believed that the only way the country could get out of this was to have someone with audacity, [**Cuba needed**] **someone capable of violent action**.

  ------------------------(Elaborate)

- Castro was in school all this time (he went **to school partially here in the US and partially in Cuba**), he became a lawyer, trying to figure out that something has to be done...

- **Castro's idea was at first to have democracy**, to restore the rule of law, he had a well-planned economy.

- **A writer states** that when Castro reunited with his brother and other activists, they came to the realization that American influence in Cuba was

25

so profound that he could not make the revolution, he could not make the changes he wanted to make unless he removed the United States from Cuba's economy and society.

- He said that **Castro had to go against the United States**, that was the only way he believed he was going to change the country.

- And that's what he did, after several meetings between activists, and with an Anti-American, Pro-Communist named Che Guevara, and his brother Raul, they took over the country and made it communist.

- The problem started right there.

- [An important point, when Castro took over the country, he several times declared that anyone who did not agree with his way of governing the country, if they wanted to leave Cuba, they could go... Cubans freely left by the tens of thousands to the US.]

-------------------------(Elaborate)

B- The five steps recommended by the New Haven School

I- Observation, Clarification, and Delimitation of the problem

a. The problem

- Cuba turned into communism, **the US put economic sanctions against Cuba.**

- It placed an **embargo on exports** to Cuba, and **restrictions on Cuban travel and commerce** for all people and companies under the United States jurisdiction, and an **embargo banning even food and medicine**.

- This went for decades. The embargo had some negative and some positive effects.

b. Causes and effects of the embargo

- Negative aspects of the embargo in Cuba:

1- The exchange of the market being closed, they were not able to travel and expand;

2- People in some parts of the country were already in extreme poverty, now with the embargo, most people haven't been able to eat properly;

3- Cubans in Cuba have been involuntarily dispersed from their family – which led them to the boat system;

4- Cuban economy collapsed mostly because of the embargo.

5- When the economy collapsed, it forced young women and men into prostitution. Prostitution rate rose very high. An author says it's an anomaly in Cuba; it was never like that before.

- Positive aspects of the embargo in Cuba:

1- Despite the embargo, Cuba managed to better the peoples' education; the population became highly educated; a large number of people attained graduate degrees

- Most likely Castro created a good school system, because many people from different developed countries go to Cuba for their higher education. According to UNESCO, their literacy rate became effectively 100%;

2- Best doctors in the world are in Cuba or from Cuba; they became the most humanitarian people, helping and curing people everywhere;

3- Despite the embargo, Cuba managed to keep its economy afloat with aid he's getting from the USSR;

4- During the Castro regime there is no homeless in Cuba, the system doesn't allow it to happen;

5- Cuba is very religious/catholic, stays in close contact with Rome; they strictly go by what the Bible say, consumption of alcohol is strictly controlled, they have a very low crime rate;

6- Tourism: Canadians, Haitians, Mexicans, many people from other counties are regularly visiting Cuba. Exportation of the Cuban music is extremely wide within... CDs are made in Canada, while the US refused to deal with them;

7- Managed to fix old American cars and somehow resell them back to America through Mexico as antiques;

8- Became number one sellers of cigars; ...best cigars in the world;

It Also have some positive aspects in the US
-------------------------(Elaborate)

- Positive aspects in the US

1- Cuban Americans have created a wealthy, successful, politically influential immigrant society;

2- Many immigrants rebuilt their lives, they recreated and reinterpreted Cuban culture in a new homeland;

3- They transformed Miami into a Latin American city-they brought a Latin flavor to America.

II- Identification, Classification, of Conflicting Claims

a. Who are the claimants and what do they claim and why?

The claimant, the United States for decades:

- They wanted to expand to Cuba,

- They wanted to preoccupy Cuba

- They wanted to establish a Democratic system in Cuba, as a communist country, it poses a threat to the US;

- They wanted to have Cuba into their possession for its huge plantations of sugar cane and tobacco, it's a close and great place to grow cash with cheap labor

- Well some people think it's because America is greedy

------- Now the US wants to release the sanctions.

b. What do the Advocate institutions say about that?

1- The UN General Assembly adopted a resolution calling for an end to the economic, commercial, and financial blockade imposed by the United States against Cuba.

2- Other organizations?

Within the 193-nation assembly, 188 countries elected for the nonbinding resolution, titled "Necessity of Ending the Economic, Commercial and Financial Embargo imposed by the United States of America against Cuba."

III- Past trends in Decision and Conditioning Factors

- The US planned several invasions to overthrow Castro's administration, but none of them were successful...

a. The different invasions

1- Invasion at <u>Bay of Pigs</u>
2- Operations 'hot plate'
3- Operation full house
4- Operation 'bugle call'
5- Operation Raincoat
6- Operation 'oplan 312' and 'oplan 316'

7- Operation Northwoods (Plot to blow up a US ship in Guantanamo Bay and blame Cuba and have a US military intervention in Cuba).

8- Operation Mongoose ("Possible Actions to Provoke, Harass or Disrupt Cuba." It was a plan to create incident which would have the appearance of an attack on US facilities in Cuba, which would provide an excuse for the US military to invade and overthrow Castro.)

9- Operation Dirty Trick (A plot to blame Castro)

10- A plot to make it appear that Cuba had attacked a member of the Organization of American States (OAS)

11- A plot to bribe one of Castro's subordinate commanders to initiate an attack on the US Navy base at Guantanamo.

12- Body of Secrets

13- Operation Pretext – A plan to create a war between Cuba and another Latin American country so that the US would intervene.

14- 'Destruction Operations" – President Kennedy approved the CIA plan to attack a large oil refinery and storage facilities... A plan to kill Castro.

15- President Nixon's directed the CIA to intensify covert operations against Cuba.

16- Under Nixon's government – A plot to attack fishing boats, embassies and Cuban offices overseas, and the bombing of a Cuban airliner killing all 73 passengers.

17- Bombings in Cuba

b. How the world responded to these conflicting claims Past and Present

1- The UN, for a long time, condemned Cuba – Now they are being controversial. They condemn the decades-long U.S. economic embargo against Cuba.

2- Some people think that the US should not be backing down because it will make the US appear weak, they believe that simply the Cuban elite will benefit from the release of the embargo.

3- George W. Bush administration added new, more severe restrictions to the embargo and increased penalties on Cuba.

4- On the other hand, the Clinton administration signed an order to lift some travel restrictions and to allow a Western Union office to open in Havana. He said that "the embargo was a foolish failure... because it allowed Castro to demonize the United States for decades." He added that 'anyone with half a brain could see the embargo was counterproductive.'

5- In 2004, President Obama (senator at that time) stated that the Cuban embargo has now been there since he was born,...It is now time to acknowledge that that particular policy has failed.

6- In 2011, President Obama lifted restrictions on travel and allowed transfers of funds, and also asked to release political prisoners.

7- The European Union had always condemned the embargo.

c. Legislative and Public Policy Framework

1- In 2013, the UN passed a resolution condemning the embargo. The vote was 188/2, only Israel supported the US policy;

2- On Dec. 17, 2014, for the first time in the history, President Obama declared a re-establishment of full diplomatic relations with Cuba.

d. Laws

1- On May 29, 2015, the United States formally removed from Cuba the list of state sponsors of terrorism.

2- On July 1, 2015, President Obama has agreed to formally reestablish diplomatic relations with Cuba and to reopen embassies.

3- July 20, 2015, as a sign of renewed diplomatic relations, the Cuban flag was raised over Washington DC embassy for the first time after 54 years.

4- On Aug. 14, 2015, US Secretary of State John Kerry traveled to Cuba to hoist the American flag over the US embassy there.

IV- Projection or Prediction of future trends

Before projecting, we need to find out what could be the reasons or motives for this whole scenario – why? why now? – unclear reasons

1- Could be: Since the US tried to intervene so many times, never worked, now they want to do the opposite.

2- Could be: The US wants to apply the system "Je t'embrasse pour mieux t'ettouffer" – Sun Tzu, in The Art of War

3- Could be: That Cuba has the best doctors, and best at other things-why don't we all get along and share –

In response to the questions, regardless of what could be the reasons, the embargo should be released. It will benefit both countries culturally, economically, and more...

V- Alternatives and Recommendations in the Global Common Interest

- While the embargo should be released, America should be open-minded to ALL kinds of government, and stop thinking that only his is best. Other options sometimes may culturally fit other places better.

- America should also now accept the fact that embargo is not a solution... Embargo should be seen as a crime. When a country already so poor, so underdeveloped, not being able to produce by itself, get sanctioned by a so powerful country, knowing that the sanctioned country with its people will be destroyed because of it, is a crime against humanity.

- Embargo should be seen as a human right violation, it punishes people for their freedom of choice, cutting off relationships and closing economic doors with the idea that the people might starve to death because of just one person's idea... that is a crime, that is a violation of human right....

- America should release the embargo, put aside all differences and make peace with one another.

Conclusion: (Personal input) Some people saw Castro as a villain but some saw him as a hero, or a champion of social justice. I think that he is a hero and a champion, because he stood up to the United States and survived. The embargo was supposed to have negative effects, but Castro turned it into positive. —A brief comparison between the embargo in Haiti and in Cuba, when Haiti had an about 3 years of embargo, Haiti didn't know what to do and how to handle it, it totally devastated the whole country; but Castro 'stood at the center of the dangerous game the United States,' and 'managed to turn his island into a launching pad for the projection of his leadership throughout the world.' Castro is a hero. Period.

PART III

THE DRAFT
on
An analysis on
The Economic Sanctions
& the Cuban Embargo

1

International Law in the 21st century
A Research Paper for a Seminar

What is God's perspective on government?

What does God say about politics?

"Let everyone be subject to the governing authorities, for there is no authority except that which God has established. The authorities that exist have been established by God. Consequently, whoever rebels against the authority is rebelling against what God has instituted, and those who do so will bring judgment on themselves." (Romans 13:1-2 NIV)

"Do nothing out of selfish ambition or vain conceit. Rather, in humility value others above yourselves, not looking to your own interests but each of you to the interests of the others. In your relationships with one another, have the same mindset as Christ Jesus: Who, being in very nature God, did not consider equality with God something to be used to his own advantage; rather, he made himself nothing by taking the very nature[b] of a servant, being made in human likeness." (Philippians 2:3-7 NIV)

CONTENTS

A- Introduction 45

B- A Brief Historical Background Of Cuban Politics............45

C- The Five Steps Recommended By The New Haven
   School..50
    I- Observation, Clarification, and Delimitation of the
      problem 50
      a)- The problem 50
      b)- Cause and effects of the embargo 51
         1- Negative aspects of the embargo......................51
         2- Positive aspects of the embargo.......................61
         3- Positive aspects in the US.................................63

    II- Identification and Classification of Conflicting
      Claims...63
      a)- Who are the claimants and what do they
         claim and why? 63
      b)- What do the Advocate institutions say about
         that? 64
         1- The UN 64
         2- Other organizations 64
      c)- The claimants and non-claimants perspectives....65
         1- The United States 65
         2- The UN...65

3- Proponents of the embargo...........................65
4- Opponents of the embargo 66
d)- The claimants' bases of power 66
1- Its Geography 67
2- Its People..67
3- Education..67
4- Leadership 68
5- Stability... 68
6- The Wars.. 68
7- Weapons... 68

III- Past trends 69
a)- Past trends in decision and conditioning factors..69
1- The different invasions.............................70
2- How everyone else responded to these
conflicting claims in the past...........................70
3- How other scholars responded and my
personal input 72
b)- Legislative and Public Policy Framework.............76
c)- Laws...78

IV- Future trends 91
a)- What the US seems to be going to decide 91
b)- What could be the reason(s) or motive(s) 92
c) Possible Projection or Prediction........................94

V- Alternatives and Recommendations in the Global
Common Interest 95

D- Conclusion 98

Other Reference...101

A- INTRODUCTION

The purpose of this analysis is to find a solution for the U.S.-Cuba 'awkward' relationship regarding the ongoing sanctions the US put on Cuba decades ago when Fidel Castro, the Cuban leader, refused to abide by the American democratic system, decided instead to have his country under the communist system. Many thinkers have tried to come up with solutions for the two countries, but their relationship has remained just about the same for over 53 years now.

Today American authorities are trying to change things and want to release the sanctions.[1] The key questions are, is it a good idea? What would be the outcome? And then, why? Why now? This analysis will use the five step process of the New Haven School in order to find an answer to those questions by starting to give a brief historical background of Cuban politics. The process consists of the delimination of the problem, the identification of the conflicting claims, the test of past decisions and its conditioning factors, the projection of future decisions, and the appraisal of past and future decisions including the recommendations. Last, this analysis will conclude with my personal thoughts.

B- A BRIEF HISTORICAL BACKGROUND OF CUBAN POLITICS

Before Castro, Cuba used to be seen as "the brothel of the Western hemisphere" — it was a playground for adventurous Americans, an island occupied by people whose main activity was to cater to American tourists at Havana's luxurious hotels,

---

[1] Leogrande, William. "Cuba and the Revolution." Interview Excerpts. PBS Online, 21 Dec. 2004. Web. 24 Feb. 2016.
    ^http://www.pbs.org/wgbh/amex/castro/sfeature/sf_experts.html^.

beaches and casinos.[2] Cuba was one of the most advanced and flourishing countries in Latin America. Cuba's capital, Havana, was a sparkling and dynamic city. However, there was a 'libertinage' going on there, as it was like a free country where people were doing whatever they wanted as far as prostitution, consumption of alcohol, and crimes. Cuba was another Las Vegas, with the drinking, gambling, mostly by the Americans, as they were deliberately going in and out.[3]

Then there were the mafia.[4] In the movie Scarface, an American crime drama film, the author describes Cuba by telling the story of a Cuban refugee who arrives in Miami with nothing and rises to become a powerful drug lord. The film shows that tones of cocaine were coming to Cuba from Colombia through Miami. It portrays Cuba as a place embedded with excessive violence, profanity and graphic drug usage. The film is considered by some people to be one of the best movies portraying Cuba and has resulted since in many culture references.[5]

On the other hand, there were profound inequalities in Cuban society – between the city and the countryside and between whites and blacks. In the countryside, some Cubans lived in terrible poverty. There was an army of unemployed people, perpetually in debt, living on the margins of survival.

---

[2] Bleys, Rudi. "Images of Ambiente." Homotextuality and Latin American Art 1810 – today: 37. Print. 2000

[3] William Leogrande. "Fidel Castro and History." PBS. PBS, 21 Dec. 2004. Web. 25 Feb. 2016.
    ^http://www.pbs.org/wgbh/amex/castro/sfeature/sf_experts.html^.

[4] Latell, Brian. "Fidel Castro and History." Interview Excerpts. PBS Online, 21 Dec. 2004. Web. 24 Feb. 2016.
    ^http://www.pbs.org/wgbh/amex/castro/sfeature/sf_experts.html^.

[5] Scarface. By Oliver Stone. Perf. Al Pacino and Michelle Pfeiffer. Universal Studios Entertainment, 1983. DVD.

Many poor peasants were seriously malnourished and hungry. Neither health care nor education reached those countryside Cubans. Illiteracy was widespread, and those lucky enough to attend school rarely made it past the first or second grades. Clusters of graveyards dotted the main highways, marking the spots where people died waiting for transportation to the nearest hospitals and clinics.[6]

William M. LeoGrande, Professor of Government and a specialist in Latin American politics, states in his book, Back Channel to Cuba, that Castro was motivated by two sets of important values. One was the drive for social equality which is social justice within Cuba; as Castro saw the horrible inconsistencies between rich and poor, urban and rural, men and women, black and white, he felt obligated to do something about it. The second set of principle, professor LeoGrande asserts, had to do with Cuba's relationship to the U.S.; he said that Castro saw the history of Cuba being conquered by U.S. power, both economic and political; he then formed an objective of the revolution to free Cuba from that U.S. domination.[7]

Professor LeoGrande goes on and states that, when in 1959 Castro said, this is going to be a true revolution, he imagined that Castro was referring to carry reforms that will address the economic and social inequalities of Cuban society; a revolution that promises to get beyond the corruption that's been so traditional that democratic governments did not address.[8]

---

[6] Leogrande, William. "Cuba and the Revolution." Interview Excerpts. PBS Online, 21 Dec. 2004. Web. 24 Feb. 2016.
^http://www.pbs.org/wgbh/amex/castro/sfeature/sf_experts.html^.
[7] LeGrande, William M. Back Channel to Cuba: The Hidden History of Negotiations between Washington and Havana. 2nd ed. Chapel Hill: U. of North Carolina, 2014.
[8] The Cuban Revolution (1957-1958). http://www.latinamericanstudies. org/rebels-in-oriente-3.htm

In addition, racism destroyed Cuban society. The island's private clubs and beaches were segregated. Even President Fulgencio Batista, a mulatto, was denied membership in one of Havana's most exclusive clubs. Cuba's social problems were compounded by a violent, hectic, disorganized and corrupt political history. Since their independence, Cuba always had bad governments. It was a bloody and costly struggle to achieve independence from Spain, but all the good leaders were being killed. Cuba was a democrat country for about 12 years, with free elections, but it was a democracy spoiled by corruption and political violence – There were action groups or gangs who shot their way through politics.[9]

Castro was in school all this time; he went to school partially in the US and partially in Cuba; he became a lawyer, trying to figure out that something has to be done. Castro's idea was at first to have democracy, to restore the rule of law, he had a well-planned economy. Professor Marifeli Perez Stable in a debate on Cuba and the Revolution, states that six months before the revolution, Castro wrote to his best friend and confidant Celia Sanchez, that once the revolution is over "I will start what to me is a much longer and bigger war, the war I am going to wage against the Americans. I realize this will be my true destiny."[10]

Professor Stable explains that when Castro reunited with his brother and other activists, they came to the realization that American influence in Cuba was so profound that he could not make the revolution. She affirms that, after Castro came in contact with the writings of nationalist professors while he was a student at the University of Havana, Castro believed

---

[9] The Cuban Revolution (1957-1958). http://www.latinamericanstudies. org/rebels-in-oriente-3.htm
[10] The Cuban Revolution (1957-1958). http://www.latinamericanstudies. org/rebels-in-oriente-3.htm

that Cuba's destiny had been stopped by the intervention of the US, and that the Platt Amendment and the U.S. economic domination had merged to strip Cuba of its independence and national pride.[11]

In Castro's beliefs system, Professor Stable adds, Cuba's political failure was America's fault, and that Castro thought he could not make the changes he wanted to make unless he removed the US from Cuba's economy and society. She said that Castro had to go against the United States, that was the only way he believed he was going to change the country. And that's what he did.[12]

After several meetings between activists, and with an Anti-American, Pro-Communist named Che Guevara, and his brother Raul, Stable affirms, they took over the country and made it communist. The problem started right there.[13]

The three most powerful leaders of the Cuban revolutionary, Fidel Castro, Raul Castro, and Che Guevara, so proud of their work has declared their willingness to help other revolutionaries "in any corner of the world."[14]

---

[11] American Experience: Fidel Castro. (Fidel Castro and History). December 21, 2004 http://www.pbs.org/wgbh/amex/castro/sfeature/sf_experts.html
[12] American Experience: Fidel Castro. (Fidel Castro and History). December 21, 2004 http://www.pbs.org/wgbh/amex/castro/sfeature/sf_experts.html
[13] American Experience: Fidel Castro. (Fidel Castro and History). December 21, 2004 http://www.pbs.org/wgbh/amex/castro/sfeature/sf_experts.html
[14] Amnesty International September 2009 Index: AMR 25/007/2009

C- THE FIVE STEPS RECOMMENDED BY THE NEW HAVEN SCHOOL

I- Observation, Clarification, and Delimitation of the problem

a)- The problem

Cuba turned into communism in 1959, and in 1960, for nearly half a century, the US has unilaterally imposed economic, commercial, and financial sanctions against Cuba. It placed an embargo on exports to Cuba, and restrictions on Cuban travel and commerce for all people and companies under the United States jurisdiction, and an embargo banning even food and medicine.

First it completely stopped sugar cane imports from Cuba in response to Cuba's nationalization of foreign property and businesses, the majority owned by US nationals.[15] Then, the embargo limited Cuba's ability to the importation of medicines, medical equipments and the latest technologies, some of which are indispensable to cure life-threatening diseases and maintaining Cuba's public health programs.[16]

---

[15] In the late 1950s, US interests owned, among other things, 25 per cent of Cuba's land (75 per cent of all arable land), 50 per cent of the sugar industry (Cuba was the world's third largest sugar producer), and 90 per cent of the transportation and electrical services. Source: US Department of Agriculture, Cuba's Food and Agriculture Situation Report, March 2008, http://www.fas.usda.gov/itp/cuba/CubaSituation0308.pdf.

[16] Domínguez, Jorge I. Professor. Cuba: Order and Revolution. 1978. 10 Trading With the Enemy Act of 1917. US Code, Title 50, Appendix – War and National Defense, (ACT OCT. 6, 1917, CH. 106, 40 STAT. 411). Available at: http://uscode.house.gov/pdf/2001/2001usc50a.pdf

b)- Cause and effects of the embargo

1- Negative aspects of the embargo

Although international law including human rights law provide limits to the imposition of sanctions, but the severity, the intense, and the continuous imposition of the embargo have provoked some negative impacts that became persistent in the social, economic, and environmental Cuban population.[17] The exchange of the market being closed, they were not able to travel and expand. People in some parts of the country were already in extreme poverty, now with the embargo, most people haven't been able to eat properly; Cubans in Cuba have been involuntarily dispersed from their family – which led them to the boat system.

Furthermore, Cuban economy collapsed mostly because of the embargo; when the economy collapsed, it forced young women and men into more prostitution. Prostitution rate rose very high. Professor Jorge Domínguez, a professor of Latin American politics at Havard University, says it's an anomaly in Cuba; it was never like that before, he adds.[18] The embargo negatively impacted the economic and social rights of the Cuban population.

It's been 19 years since the UN Secretary-General has been documenting the negative impacts of the US embargo on

---

[17] Domínguez, Jorge I. Professor. Cuba: Order and Revolution. 1978. 10 Trading With the Enemy Act of 1917. US Code, Title 50, Appendix – War and National Defense, (ACT OCT. 6, 1917, CH. 106, 40 STAT. 411). Available at: http://uscode.house.gov/pdf/2001/2001usc50a.pdf

[18] Domínguez, Jorge I. Professor. Cuba: Order and Revolution. 1978. 10 Trading With the Enemy Act of 1917. US Code, Title 50, Appendix – War and National Defense, (ACT OCT. 6, 1917, CH. 106, 40 STAT. 411). Available at: http://uscode.house.gov/pdf/2001/2001usc50a.pdf

Cuba. In one of the last reports of the Human Rights Council, the Personal Representative of the United Nations High Commissioner for Human Rights on the situation of human rights in Cuba expressed the effects of the embargo on the economic, social and cultural rights of the Cuban people and called it "disastrous".[19]

Article 12(1) of the International Covenant on Economic, Social and Cultural Rights (ICESCR) recognizes that the right to health holds a wide range of socio-economic factors that support conditions in which people can have a healthy life, and expands to the fundamental determinants of health, such as food and nutrition, housing, access to safe drinking water and adequate sanitation, safe and healthy working conditions, and a healthy environment.

Article 12(2) further affirms that "the steps to be taken... shall include those necessary for... the creation of conditions which would assure to all medical service and medical attention in the event of sickness." The right to health is not limited to the right to, but includes, health care. Article 25 of the Universal Declaration of Human Rights (UDHR) identifies the right of "everyone... to a standard of living adequate for the health and well-being of himself and of his family, including food, clothing, housing and medical care and necessary social services..."

The US embargo has been a major factor in delaying improvement on meeting the MDGs (the United Nations

---

[19] See A/HRC/4/12, paragraph 7. Amnesty International last visit to Cuba took place in 1988. Ever since, Amnesty International's repeated requests for an authorization to visit Cuba have been denied by the Cuban government. http://bangkok.ohchr.org/news/

Millennium Development Goals), particularly in further reducing infant and maternal mortality rates.[20]

The US Government Accountability Office 2000 report says that US medical and pharmaceutical exports to Cuba amounted to US$120,000 which is 0.04 % of total exports to Cuba. Exports of licensed humanitarian items, including donated medicine and medical products, amounted to US$6.9 million which is 1.98% of total exports to Cuba.[21] However, on October 28, 2000, the UN passed the Trade Sanctions Reform and Export Enhancement Act, which alleviated and eased exports of agricultural products and medicine to Cuba, the total US exports to Cuba from 2001 to 2008 increased from US$7.2 million to US$711 million, according to the figures from the US Census Bureau.[22]

The Department of Commerce is the branch that authorizes the use of License Exception Agricultural Commodities for exports of agricultural products. The license was issued to Cuba. However, exports of medicine and medical devices to Cuba are not eligible for License Exception Agricultural Commodities and have been and remain to be subject of the requirements for the Cuban Democracy Act. The easing of exports of agricultural products has only addressed food shortages and only contributes towards the realization of the right to food for Cubans; the export of medicines and medical equipment is

---

[20] UNICEF, Background on Cuba: http://www.unicef.org/infobycountry/cuba.html.

[21] Obtained from United States Government Accountability Office, Economic Sanctions, and Agencies Face Competing Priorities in Enforcing the U.S. Embargo on Cuba, November 2007; Table 6, Composition of U.S. exports to Cuba in 2000, p. 30. The report is available at:
http://www.gao.gov/new.items/d0880.pdf.

[22] US Department of treasury: http://www.treasury.gov/resource-center/sanctions/Programs/Pages/tsra.aspx

persisting to be severely limited and has a negative impact on the progressive realization of the right to health.

The Department of Commerce, in its 2008 Report on Foreign Policy-Based Export Controls, states about the restrictions in exporting goods and medicines to Cuba that: "The Department generally denies license applications for exports or re-exports to Cuba. However, the Department considers applications for the following on a case-by-case basis:-exports from foreign countries of non-strategic, foreign-made products containing 20 percent or less U.S.-origin parts, components, or materials, provided the exporter is not a U.S.-owned or controlled foreign firm in a third country; The Department reviews applications for exports of donated and commercially supplied medicine or medical devices to Cuba on a case-by-case basis, pursuant to the provisions of Section 6004 of the Cuban Democracy Act of 1992."[23]

Restrictions are also placed on donations of medicine and medical equipments by the US authorities. An export license is still obligatory even when the donation is for humanitarian purposes. In June 2007, officials at the Maine-Quebec (Canada) border stopped and had a shipment of medical donations for Cuba pushed back. The medicines had been gathered and assembled by the Quebec-Cuba Friendship Caravan and were supposed to be transferred to Cuba by the 18th Caravan of the Pastors for Peace Organization.[24] In preceding years, US authorities stopped the Caravan despite the fact that it was crossing the border into Mexico from where the final shipment

---

[23] US Department of Commerce, Bureau of Industry and Security, 2008 Report on Foreign Policy-Based Export Controls, p. 34: https://www.bis.doc.gov/index.php/forms-documents/doc view/649-bis-foreign-policy-report-2008

[24] Latin American and Caribbean Economic System, Follow up report on the application of the Helms-Burton law, 2007-2008, p. 5.

was supposed to take place and confiscated medicines and medical materials.[25]

According to the Personal Representative of the High Commissioner for Human Rights, the restrictions of the embargo imposed Cuba to access to medicines, new scientific and medical technology, food, chemical water treatment and electricity.[26] The negative impact of the US embargo on the Cuban health care system and on the right to health of Cubans during the 1990s has been recognized in the 1997 report of the American Association for World Health (AAWH).[27]

The 300-page document is one of the most comprehensive studies on the issue. According to a fact-finding mission to Cuba by the AAWH, the embargo was the fundamental reason of the rise of malnutrition in Cuba which affected particularly women and children, poor water quality, due to lack of access to medicines and medical supplies, and limited the exchange of medical and scientific information, because of travel restrictions and currency regulations. The AAWH established that "a humanitarian catastrophe has been averted only because the Cuban government has maintained a high level of budgetary support for a health care system designed to deliver primary and preventive health care to all of its citizens... Even so, the U.S. embargo of food and the de facto embargo on

---

[25] See Pastors for Peace website: http://www.ifconews.org/
[26] Human Rights Council, Situation of Human Rights in Cuba, Report submitted by the Personal Representative of the High Commissioner for Human Rights, Christine Chanet, A/HRC/4/12, para 7.
[27] American Association for World Health, Denial of Food and Medicine: The Impact of the U.S. Embargo on Health & Nutrition in Cuba, March 1997. Available at:
   http://www.medicc.org/resources/documents/embargo/The%20 impact%20of%20the%20U.S.%20Embargo%20on%20Health%20&%20 Nutrition%20in%20Cuba.pdf

medical supplies have wreaked havoc with the island's model primary health care system."[28]

The Cuban Democracy Act was a bill offered by US Congressman R. Torricelli and passed in 1992 which barred foreign-based subsidiaries of U.S. companies from trading with Cuba, travel to Cuba by U.S. citizens, and family remittances to Cuba. The act stated that the government of Castro has demonstrated consistent disregard for internationally accepted standards of democratic values, adding there is no sign that the Castro regime is prepared to make any considerable concessions to democracy or to undertake any form of democratic opening.

Congressman Torricelli stated that the act was intended to "wreck havoc on that island. The bill was passed; the sales of medicines were exempt from the embargo. However, access to medicines became practically impossible for Cuba. Every export of medicine required that the President of the USA certify, and approve it, and that all components of a shipment of medical products to Cuba were used for the purpose intended.[29]

The Cuban Liberty and Democratic Solidarity (Libertad) Act of 1996 (Helms–Burton Act, is a United States federal law which strengthens and continues the United States embargo against Cuba. It penalizes non-US companies and nationals for trading with Cuba. Although commercial opportunities are available to Cuba throughout the rest of the Americas, Europe, Asia, and elsewhere, the Helms-Burton Act has restrained non-US medical companies, therefore limiting Cuba's access to medicines, medical equipment and technologies.

[28] American Association for World Health, Denial of Food and Medicine: The Impact of the U.S. Embargo on Health & Nutrition in Cuba, March 1997, p. i.
[29] Kirkpatrick, Anthony F. "Role of the USA in shortage of food and medicine in Cuba". The Lancet, 1996, Vol. 348, p. 1489-91.

Cubans are denied the latest generation of equipment and medicine, available in some cases only from US companies or at prohibitively high prices through third countries.[30] The World Health Organization reported from Cuba, "lack of diagnostic materials and equipment, replacement parts, surgical supplies and drugs hinders the operations of emergency services and care for patients in serious condition. The resources for treating patients who need this type of care, adults and children alike, are limited. In the case of patients with psychiatric disorders, state-of-the-art drugs are unavailable."[31]

In July 2004, a US biotechnology firm located in California settled a civil penalty with the Office of Foreign Asset Control (OFAC) for a total of US$168,500. The firm had voluntarily released to OFAC the shipment of three vaccines for infants and children between 1999 and 2002 from its factories in Germany and Italy while the company held a license to export just one vaccine through UNICEF.[32] The vaccines included those for polio, hemophilic influenza, flu, rabies and a vaccine for measles, mumps and rubella.[33]

[30] Reported by the Economic Commission for Latin America and the Caribbean, in Necessity of ending the economic, commercial and financial embargo imposed by the United States of America against Cuba, Report of the Secretary-General, A/63/93, 1 August 2008, p. 85.
[31] Report from the World Health Organization in Necessity of ending the economic, commercial and financial embargo imposed by the United States of America against Cuba, Report of the Secretary-General, A/63/93, 1 August 2008, p. 110, paragraph 3
[32] See OFAC Civil Penalties Enforcement Information, Archive of 2004 Enforcement Information: http://www.treas.gov/offices/enforcement/ofac/civpen/penalties/06042004.pdf ; and Silber, Judy. "Chiron fined for exports to Cuba". Contra Costa Times, 9 July 2004, cited in Richard Garfield, "Health care in Cuba and the manipulation of humanitarian imperatives", The Lancet, 11 September 2004, Vol. 364, p. 1007.
[33] Medical Education Cooperation with Cuba, Medicc Review, "Washington Fines US Company for Selling Children's Vaccines to Cuba", Vol. 6, No. 1,

In November 2005, the Bureau of Industry and Security, Department of Commerce forced a civil penalty of US$37,500 on a company located in Massachusetts specialized in medical equipment, for "attempting to export and conspiring to export X ray film processors to Cuba via Canada without the required license and with knowledge that a violation would occur".[34]

UNICEF reported that Cuba was incapable to trade in nutritional products intended for children and for consumption at schools, hospitals and day care centers. This had an unfavorable effect on the health and nutritional status of the population and is believed to be a causal factor in the high prevalence of iron deficiency anemia which in 2007 affected 37.5 per cent of children under three years old.[35] Children's health was also put at risk by a decision from syringe suppliers to cancel an order for 3 million disposable syringes by UNICEF's Global Alliance for Vaccines and Immunization when it became known that the units were destined for the implementation of the program in Cuba.

The number of children afflicted by heart conditions who are waiting for appropriate treatment at a pediatric hospital has increased after Cuba was unable to buy from the US-based companies the necessary medical equipment for their treatment. The companies refused to negotiate with Cuba

---

2004. Available at:
    http://www.medicc.org/publications/medicc_review/1004/pages/ headlines_in_cuban_health4.html.
[34] United States Government Accountability Office, Economic Sanctions, Agencies Face Competing Priorities in Enforcing the U.S. Embargo on Cuba, November 2007, p. 51.
[35] Report by UNICEF in Necessity of ending the economic, commercial and financial embargo imposed by the United States of America against Cuba, Report of the Secretary-General, A/63/93, p. 94, para 4.

because of the restrictions set by the US embargo.[36] The World Health Organization informed that "lack of access to products manufactured by United States companies such as St. Jude Medical, Boston Scientific and Amplatzer inhibits the provision of proper care to critically ill patients who require a pacemaker, St. Jude prosthetic valves or septal occluders, forcing their treatment with alternative, riskier surgical techniques."[37]

Shortage of medication and equipment has as well affected treatment for children being treated at the National Institute of Oncology and Radiology. According to UNICEF, it has been impossible to purchase a positron emission tomography/ computerized tomography (PET/CT) scanner, a state-of-the-art piece of medical tools required for cure that is made by only three manufacturers worldwide, all unauthorized to negotiate with Cuba.[38]

Programs to prevent and fight HIV/AIDS have also endured from the embargo eventhough they are implemented by UN agencies. In 2006, the purchase of antiretroviral drugs by UNICEF in support of the Global Fund to Fight AIDS, Tuberculosis and Malaria was delayed, because major suppliers to UNICEF could not offer their products for the implementation of the Fund programs in Cuba because of the US embargo. According to UN reports, transactions with more

---

[36] Necessity of ending the economic, commercial and financial embargo imposed by the United States of America against Cuba, Report of the Secretary-General, A/63/93, p. 95.

[37] Report by the World Health Organization in Necessity of ending the economic, commercial and financial embargo imposed by the United States of America against Cuba, Report of the Secretary-General, A/63/93, p. 110, para 3.

[38] Report by UNICEF in Necessity of ending the economic, commercial and financial embargo imposed by the United States of America against Cuba, Report of the Secretary-General, A/63/93, p. 94, para 4.

far-off suppliers result in an increase in prices and delays in procurement of antiretrovirals.[39]

In August 2007, media reports expressed that the US Treasury Department had refused to renew a license to health organization Population Services International (PSI) to export condoms to Cuba for distribution to groups at high risk of contracting HIV infection.[40]

Access to new drugs could be life-saving for many Cubans living with HIV/AIDS. However, Cuba cannot import the latest antiretrovirals from the USA or from other countries due to patent restrictions. The Joint United Nations Program on HIV/AIDS reported in 2008 that Abbott was prevented from selling two drugs for AIDS treatment — Ritonavir and Liponavir + Ritonavir — resulting in a six fold increase in price to acquire them from another manufacturer. Similarly, Gilead replied that it could not supply the antiretroviral drug Tenofovir because it would require an export license from the United States.[41]

The UN Development Program (UNDP) reported delays in acquiring equipment to measure viral load and flow cytometers to verify CD4 cell count, because of difficulties forced by the embargo in the purchasing process.[42]

---

[39] Necessity of ending the economic, commercial and financial embargo imposed by the United States of America against Cuba, Report of the Secretary-General, A/61/132, 8 August 2006, p. 73.

[40] Latin American and Caribbean Economic System, Follow up report on the application of the Helms-Burton law, 2007-2008, p. 5.

[41] Necessity of ending the economic, commercial and financial embargo imposed by the United States of America against Cuba, Report of the Secretary-General, A/62/92, 3 August 2007, p. 89.

[42] Report by the UNDP in Necessity of ending the economic, commercial and financial embargo imposed by the United States of America against Cuba, Report of the Secretary-General, A/63/93, 1 August 2008, p. 102, para. 10.

Health and health services don't only depend on supplies of medicine, but they also depend on functioning water and sanitation infrastructure, on electricity and other functioning equipment such as X-ray facilities or refrigerators to store vaccines. The financial burden and commercial barriers have led to shortages or irregular availability of drugs, medicines, equipment and spare parts. It has also delayed the renovation of hospitals, clinics and care centers for the elderly.[43]

2- Positive aspects of the embargo

Despite the embargo, Cuba managed to better the peoples' education; the population became highly educated; a large number of people attained graduate degrees. Most likely Castro created a good school system, because many people from different developed countries go to Cuba for their higher education. According to UNESCO, their literacy rate became effectively 100%. Best doctors in the world are in Cuba or from Cuba; they became the most humanitarian people, helping and curing people everywhere. Regardless of the embargo, Cuba managed to keep its economy afloat with aid he's getting from the USSR. [44]

During the Castro regime there is no homeless in Cuba, the system doesn't allow it to happen. Cuba is very religious/catholic, stays in close contact with Rome; they strictly go by what the Bible says; consumption of alcohol is strictly controlled, which leads the country to a very low crime rate. As far as tourism, Canadians, Haitians, Mexicans, many people from other counties are regularly visiting Cuba. Exportation

---

[43] Report by UNFPA, the UN Population Fund, in Necessity of ending the economic, commercial and financial embargo imposed by the United States of America against Cuba, Report of the Secretary-General
[44] American Experience: Fidel Castro. (Interview Experts). December 21, 2004 http://www.pbs.org/wgbh/amex/castro/sfeature/sf_experts.html

of the Cuban music is excessively wide within the Americas and the rest of the world. CDs are made in Canada, while the US refused to deal with them. Cubans in Cuba managed to fix old American cars and somehow resell them back to America through Mexico as antiques. Moreover, Cuba became number one seller of cigars, as it has the best cigars in the world.[45]

The UN has set a system called, The Eight Millennium Development Goals (MDGs), which range from lowering extreme poverty rates into half, to stop the spread of HIV/AIDS, to provide universal primary education, and five others, all by the end date of 2015.[46]

According to the UN Development Program, although Cuba has been challenged by the lack and in other cases absence of health supplies to stop the spread of HIV/AIDS, it has already accomplished three out of the eight Millennium Development Goals, such as universal primary education, promoting gender equality and empowering women, and reducing child mortality, and is on its way to achieve the five other goals by 2015 or is very likely to do so.[47]

---

[45] http://www.un.org/millenniumgoals/

[46] UN Development Programme, MDG Monitor,
http://www.mdgmonitor.org/country_progress.cfm?c=CUB&cd=192#, accessed 5 February 2009. Cuba is likely or on track to achieve the remaining of the Millennium Development Goals, namely: eradicate extreme poverty and hunger; improve maternal health; combat HIV/Aids, malaria and other diseases; ensure environmental sustainability; and develop a global partnership for development.

[47] UN Development Programme, MDG Monitor,
http://www.mdgmonitor.org/country_progress.cfm?c=CUB&cd=192#, accessed 5 February 2009. Cuba is likely or on track to achieve the remaining of the Millennium Development Goals, namely: eradicate extreme poverty and hunger; improve maternal health; combat HIV/Aids, malaria and other diseases; ensure environmental sustainability; and develop a global partnership for development.

3- Positive aspects in the US

We can't ignore that the embargo has caused some positive impacts right inside the United States. Just to name a few, for instance, Cuban Americans have created a wealthy, successful, politically influential immigrant society; furthermore, many immigrants rebuilt their lives, they recreated and reinterpreted Cuban culture in their new homeland; moreover, they transformed Miami into a Latin American city-they brought a Latin flavor to America.

II- Identification and Classification of Conflicting Claims

a)- Who are the claimants and what do they claim and why?

For decades, the main claimant has been the United States. What they had been wanting from Cuba is quite unclear. Some people say they wanted to expand to Cuba, or they wanted to preoccupy Cuba. Some others believe they want to establish a Democratic system in Cuba, as for the US a communist country poses a threat to the US. Many others speculate and affirm that they wanted to have Cuba into their possession for its huge plantations of sugar cane and tobacco, it's a close and great place to grow cash with cheap labor, while some others believe that it's because America is greedy, they want it all.[48] Now the US wants to release the sanctions.[49]

---

[48] http://www.pbs.org/wgbh/amex/castro/peopleevents/e_precastro.html
[49] http://www.bloomberg.com/politics/articles/2015-07-01/obama-urges-congress-to-lift-cuba-embargo-after-embassy-opened

b)- What do the Advocate institutions say about that?

1- The UN

The UN General Assembly has continually expressed disapproval of the US embargo as opposed to the Charter of the United Nations and international law. On October 2008, the UN General Assembly passed a decree re-stating for the 17th time its call on the USA to stop its embargo against Cuba.[50] That decree was implemented with 185 votes in favor, three against and two abstentions within 193 nation-assemblies. This nonbinding resolution was titled "Necessity of Ending the Economic, Commercial and Financial Embargo imposed by the United States of America against Cuba." This document reiterates previous Amnesty International recommendations calling for the lifting of the US embargo.[51]

2- Other organizations

The Inter-American Commission on Human Rights has, as well, reiterated its position regarding the embargo to be lifted, because of the impact of such sanctions on the human rights of the Cuban people.[52]

---

[50] UN General Assembly, Resolution 63/7, Necessity of ending the economic, commercial and financial embargo imposed by the United States of America against Cuba, A/RES/63/7.

[51] Inter-American Commission on Human Rights, 2008 Annual Report, Status of Human Rights in Cuba, Chapter IV, para 154, OEA/Ser.L/V/II.134, Doc. 5 rev. 1. http://www.cidh.oas.org/annualrep/2008eng/Chap4.c.eng.htm#_ftnref12, accessed October 30, 2015.

[52] The United States, Israel and Palau voted against the resolution; Marshall Islands and the Federated States of Micronesia abstained. UN General Assembly, for seventeenth consecutive year, General Assembly overwhelmingly calls for end to United States economic, trade embargo

The international community has condemned the US embargo because it believes that it violates international law, and on moral, political and economic grounds.

c)- The claimants and non-claimants perspectives

1- The United States

They wanted for decades for Cuba to become Democratic or to preoccupy Cuba, they sanctioned the Cubans for non collaborating – now why do they want to release the sanctions?

2- The UN

The UN condemned Cuba for 'Human Rights violations' – Now they are being controversial. They condemn the decades-long U.S. economic embargo against Cuba. Why?

3- Proponents of the embargo

Some people dispute that Cuba has not met what the US conditioned for lifting the embargo, which is the transitioning into democracy and the improvisation of human rights.[53]

Other proponents think that the US should not be backing down because it will make the U.S. appear weak, and that simply the Cuban elite will benefit from the release of the embargo.[54]

---

against Cuba, http://www.un.org/News/Press/docs/2008/ga10772.doc. htm, accessed October 30, 2015.

[53] Sweig, Julia E. Cuba after Communism: The Economic Reforms that are Transforming the Island. Foreign Affairs Article. July/August 2013. http://www.cfr.org/cuba/cuba-after-communism/p30991

[54] Sweig, Julia E. Cuba After Communism: The Economic Reforms that are Transforming the Island. Foreign Affairs Article. July/August 2013. http://

4- Opponents of the embargo

On the other side, opponents of the embargo think that the embargo should be lifted because the US policy has failed and has clearly not achieved its goals. They think that the sanctions have instead harmed the US economy and Cuban citizens, and prevented opportunities to promote changes and democracy in Cuba, and that instead, the embargo has hurt international opinion of the United States.[55]

d)- The claimants' bases of power

The USA is the richest, most powerful and most influential nation in the world. Even in a US vs. Rest of the World scenario, it is most unlikely to lose a war. Its economy is bigger than the economies of the next four largest nations combined. Its military budget is more than that of the next 20 nations combined. It is also no match whether one considers technology or soft power. Its values of human rights and democracy are sought by people throughout the world, not just more than any other country, but more than all of them. The consequences of that were and still are enormous. And, the East Coast by itself has more major ports than the entire rest of the Western Hemisphere.[56]

www.cfr.org/cuba/cuba-after-communism/p30992

[55] Sweig, Julia E. Cuba After Communism: The Economic Reforms that are Transforming the Island. Foreign Affairs Article. July/August 2013. http://www.cfr.org/cuba/cuba-after-communism/p30993

[56] The Geopolitics of the United States, Part 1: The Inevitable Empire Analysis. July 4, 2015 | 12:56 GM.T https://www.stratfor.com/analysis/geopolitics-united-states-part-1-inevitable-empire

1- Its Geography

The US is the 3rd largest in area and population. Since the US is guarded by two oceans and a frigid nation to the north, it never had to worry about major wars on its borders. Moreover, the US is most likely the one country that is somewhat self-sufficient in all fundamental resources. Unlike China, Japan, Germany or India, it has huge quantities of oil & gas. Unlike the Middle East, it has an abundance of water and agricultural land.[57]

2- Its People

Throughout the ages, the US' isolated location helped pick the immigrants. Other than the Mexicans, everyone else had to travel long oceans to attain the US, which made the inhabitants self-selected. "US got on to nuclear weapons and other key ideas on the back of its immigrants."[58]

3- Education

For each group of immigrants, education was a top priority. Thus, US built itself as the world's education superpower with an enormous concentration of top universities.[59]

---

[57] The Geopolitics of the United States, Part 1: The Inevitable Empire Analysis. July 4, 2015 | 12:56 GM.T https://www.stratfor.com/analysis/geopolitics-united-states-part-1-inevitable-empire
[58] The Geopolitics of the United States, Part 1: The Inevitable Empire Analysis. July 4, 2015 | 12:56 GM.T https://www.stratfor.com/analysis/geopolitics-united-states-part-1-inevitable-empire
[59] The Geopolitics of the United States, Part 1: The Inevitable Empire Analysis. July 4, 2015 | 12:56 GM.T https://www.stratfor.com/analysis/geopolitics-united-states-part-1-inevitable-empire

4- Leadership

US leaders were quite excellent by world standards. Despite all their complaining, they never had a leader like Stalin, Saddam or Mao.[60]

5- Stability

The present governments of China and India are less than 70 years old while the US' is about 240 years old and that kind of stability was lacking in most other part of the world. [61]

6- The Wars

By the start of the WWI, the US had built up a substantial economy. Although the US faced some destruction, in relative terms it got far ahead of the rest of the world. America has a strong military that has the ability and willingness to fight. It can recover quickly from disasters and crises; it has the earning power, integrated society, and very patriotic citizenry.[62]

7- Weapons

Americans have the most powerful military in the history of mankind. The Heritage Foundation released the first annual report on America's military might. The report is entitled 2015 Index of U.S. Military Strength: Assessing America's Ability to

---

[60] The Geopolitics of the United States, Part 1: The Inevitable Empire Analysis. July 4, 2015 | 12:56 GM.T https://www.stratfor.com/analysis/geopolitics-united-states-part-1-inevitable-empire

[61] The Geopolitics of the United States, Part 1: The Inevitable Empire Analysis. July 4, 2015 | 12:56 GM.T https://www.stratfor.com/analysis/geopolitics-united-states-part-1-inevitable-empire

[62] The Geopolitics of the United States, Part 1: The Inevitable Empire Analysis. July 4, 2015 | 12:56 GM.T https://www.stratfor.com/analysis/geopolitics-united-states-part-1-inevitable-empire

Provide for the Common Defense; it is modeled on Heritage's broadly successful Index of Economic Freedom.

It shows that there are 11 unbelievable arms that only America has. It reports that the Soviets exploded their first nuclear weapon in 1949, and that China revealed plans for its own stealth bomber last year, but there are still some weapons that the rest of the world doesn't have. Weapons like the MQ9 Reaper Drone, the Laser Avenger, and the ADAPTIV cloaking give U.S. troops the advantage on any battlefield around the world. The report points out that some of these weapons have been around for several years but were recently modified, and some are still in production.[63]

Then there is the economy with the ability to fund all others. There is the social with the ability of its citizens to live in harmony. Finally, there is the psychological with the ability to rally citizens.

It is impossible to deny that the US is the most powerful country in the world; they have enough education, money, and weapons. Yet, with all this power, surprisingly they could not challenge Cuba.

III- Past trends

a)- Past trends in decision and conditioning factors

This is an analysis of predispositional and environmental conditioning factors and how these factors influenced the operations (strategic interventions). The US planned several

---

[63] Johnson, Robert. Business Insider. Military & Defense: 11 Incredible Weapons That Only America Has. Nov. 10, 2011, 11:45 AM http://www. businessinsider.com/11-incredible-weapons-that-only-america-has-2011-9

invasions to overthrow Castro's administration, but none of them were successful. The attacks plots did not occur, some of them were too 'terrostic'.[64]

1- The different invasions

Invasion at Bay of Pigs in 1961 for instance was a failed military invasion of Cuba that was undertaken by the CIA and sponsored by a paramilitary group, a Cuban exiles group. There were several other ones, such as, the 1962 Operation Northwoods, that was supposed to be a plot to blow up a US ship in Guantanamo Bay and blame Cuba, and then have a US military intervention in Cuba. That one failed. Another one was the 1963 Operation Pretext, which was a plan to create a war between Cuba and another Latin American country so that the US would intervene. That one also failed. There were many other ones that failed as well.[65]

2- How everyone else responded to these conflicting claims in the past

According to the State Department Policy Planning Council, the primary danger the US faces in Castro is that Castro represents a successful defiance of the US.[66] A writer, Thomas

---

[64] US Department of the Treasury, Office of Foreign Assets Control, What you need to know about the US embargo. An overview of the Cuban Assets Control Regulations, Title 31 Part 515 of the US Code of Federal Regulations, in http://www.treas.gov/offices/enforcement/ofac/programs/cuba/cuba.pdf, accessed 30 October 2015.

[65] American Experience: Fidel Castro. (Fidel Castro and History). December 21, 2004 http://www.pbs.org/wgbh/amex/castro/sfeature/sf_experts.html

[66] Amnesty International has repeatedly called on the US government to lift its embargo against Cuba. (Index: AMR 25/017/2003), 3 June 2008; New Cuban leadership can improve human rights, 19 February 2008; Cuba: Submission to the UN Universal Periodic Review: Fourth session

Paterson writes that Cuba, as symbol and reality, challenged US authority in Latin America. President Clinton signed an executive order to lift some travel restrictions and to allow a Western Union office to open in Havana. He said that "the embargo was a foolish, pandering failure..." because It allowed Castro to demonize the U.S. for decades...' He added that 'with half a brain' could see the embargo was counterproductive."[67]

On the other hand, the George W. Bush administration added new, more severe restrictions to the embargo and increased penalties on Cuba. Former Secretary of State Hillary Clinton alleged that the Castro regime has harmed US attempts to improve relations between them. Clinton believed that Castro does not want to end the embargo and normalize with the US.[68]

President Obama (senator at that time) stated that "The Cuban embargo has failed to provide the sorts of rising standards of living, and has squeezed the innocents in Cuba and utterly failed to overthrow Castro, who has now been there since I was born. It is now time to acknowledge that particular policy has failed." A few years later, President Obama made steps to ease the Cuban embargo by lifting restrictions on travel and allowing transfers of funds, and also by asking to release political prisoners and to provide people with their basic human rights.[69]

---

of the UPR Working Group of the Human Rights Council, February 2009 (Index: AMR 25/002/2008), October 30, 2015.

[67] American Experience: Fidel Castro. (Fidel Castro and History). December 21, 2004 http://www.pbs.org/wgbh/amex/castro/sfeature/sf experts.html

[68] American Experience: Fidel Castro. (Fidel Castro and History). December 21, 2004 http://www.pbs.org/wgbh/amex/castro/sfeature/sf experts.html

[69] American Experience: Fidel Castro. (Fidel Castro and History). December 21, 2004 http://www.pbs.org/wgbh/amex/castro/sfeature/sf

US Ambassador to the UN Ronald Godard defended the sanctions as a means to support respect for human rights and basic freedoms. Godard claimed that the United States was helping the people of Cuba by sending funds in family remittances and in agricultural, medical, and humanitarian products.[70] And the European Union had always condemned the embargo.[71]

The 'warfare' against Cuba has been very strongly condemned in virtually every relevant international forum. The European Union condemned the embargo. The Judicial Commission of the normally compliant Organization of American States has declared them illegal.

3- How other scholars responded and my personal input

Some people saw Castro as a cruel dictator, or a criminal, but some saw him as a hero, a conqueror, or a champion of social justice.

James Blight, Professor of Foreign Policy Development at Balsillie School of International Affairs, states that Fidel Castro is in some ways very interesting, because "he leads a country that is $1/87^{th}$ the size of his principal mortal enemy and he not only gets away with it, but he does it with flair. He gets people to hate him but not to be able to do anything about it. He has co-opted the United States in so many ways, including getting;

---

experts.html
[70] American Experience: Fidel Castro. (Fidel Castro and History). December 21, 2004 http://www.pbs.org/wgbh/amex/castro/sfeature/sf experts.html
[71] American Experience: Fidel Castro. (Fidel Castro and History). December 21, 2004 http://www.pbs.org/wgbh/amex/castro/sfeature/sf experts.html

I would say, even now, the majority of non-U.S. citizens on his side."[72]

Ricardo Bofill, a human rights activist, thinks that Castro is "a charismatic figure. The Soviet leadership was rather grey. [Leonid] Brezhnev was a man that whispered into the microphone in the Red Square... Fidel Castro not only came with the legend of Sierra Maestra but also from having defeated the Americans at Playa Girón — that was magnified... Fidel Castro had defeated the Americans."[73]

Georgie Anne Geyer, a journalist, affirms that "Fidel Castro was able to stay in power for so many years and after so many challenges... because he was so incredibly clever — and usually much, much more clever than the people who were against him. He always knew the instincts of the other person as well as his own. He knew how to manipulate their negatives. He's not a good manipulator of positive things. He's a very strong manipulator of negatives: anti-Americanism, anti-the upper class, anti-the middle class, et cetera, et cetera... and he was attending very carefully to the United States. He knew how to... be the romantic hero."[74]

---

[72] Bossuyt, Marc: The Adverse Consequences of Economic Sanctions on the Enjoyment of Human Rights, Working Paper prepared for the Commission on Human Rights, Sub-Commission on the Promotion and Protection of Human Rights. UN Doc.E/CN.4/Sub.2/2000/33, Geneva: UN Economic and Social Council, 21 June 2000, paragraph 98-100.

[73] Bossuyt, Marc: The Adverse Consequences of Economic Sanctions on the Enjoyment of Human Rights, Working Paper prepared for the Commission On Human Rights, Sub-Commission on the Promotion and Protection of Human Rights. UN Doc.E/CN.4/Sub.2/2000/33, Geneva: UN Economic and Social Council, 21 June 2000, paragraph 98-100.

[74] Bossuyt, Marc: The Adverse Consequences of Economic Sanctions on the Enjoyment of Human Rights, Working Paper prepared for the Commission On Human Rights, Sub-Commission on the Promotion and Protection of

Armando Valladares, a political prisoner says, "Look, Fidel Castro is the First Secretary of the Communist Party; the Prime Minister; the President of the State Council; President of the Council of Ministers; the President of the Republic of Cuba; Commander in Chief of the Land, Sea and Air Forces; ... the General Supervisor of all Ministries. If he were religious, he'd also be the Pope. He's got absolute control... and when he disappears it'll be chaos."[75]

Carlos Alberto Montaner, an author, says, First of all, he thinks Fidel Castro has awakened a deep anthropological curiosity; he continues and asserts that Castro is "the bearded man dressed in military costume with a heroic history, and he militarily defeated a dictatorship. Then he is the man that confronts the United States...The legendary image that he constructs is assisted by the fact that there are very powerful feelings against the United States, the capitalist economy, and he is looked upon as a hero. The Latin American leftists perceive him as a hero that battles against adversity, and even though on occasion he has erratic behavior, his untamable character is more important than anything else."[76]

People in general have different opinions about the situation. I agree with Carlos and I think that Fidel Castro is a hero.

Human Rights. UN Doc.E/CN.4/Sub.2/2000/33, Geneva: UN Economic and Social Council, 21 June 2000, paragraph 98-100.

[75] Bossuyt, Marc: The Adverse Consequences of Economic Sanctions on the Enjoyment of Human Rights, Working Paper prepared for the Commission on Human Rights, Sub-Commission on the Promotion and Protection of Human Rights. UN Doc.E/CN.4/Sub.2/2000/33, Geneva: UN Economic and Social Council, 21 June 2000, paragraph 98-100.

[76] Bossuyt, Marc: The Adverse Consequences of Economic Sanctions on the Enjoyment of Human Rights, Working Paper prepared for the Commission On Human Rights, Sub-Commission on the Promotion and Protection of Human Rights. UN Doc.E/CN.4/Sub.2/2000/33, Geneva: UN Economic and Social Council, 21 June 2000, paragraph 98-100.

My opinion is based on results after several research, several readings, several interviews I have watched; and despites after many teachings, directions and hints from my professors, mostly from Dr. Rosa Pati, International Law Professor at St Thomas University, my thoughts and conclusions remain the same, Castro is a conqueror, and a champion. I think he is all that because he put up with the United States punishments, he subsisted and turned it into a glory. Thus, the embargo was supposed to have negative effects, but Castro turned it into positive.

I came to this terms also after a brief comparison between the embargo in Haiti and in Cuba, when Haiti had an about 3 years of embargo, Haiti didn't know what to do and how to handle it; it totally devastated the whole country.[77] But Castro "stood at the center of the dangerous game the United States..." and "...managed to turn his island into a launching pad for the projection of his leadership throughout the world." [78]

Don't get me wrong, in my perspectives Castro is not a saint, nor an angel, he may have been guilty of certain wrongdoing just like for the US, but everyone should recognize what he has accomplished. And yes, the embargo should be released while every single Cuban should enjoy.

---

[77] Bossuyt, Marc: The Adverse Consequences of Economic Sanctions on the Enjoyment of Human Rights, Working Paper prepared for the Commission On Human Rights, Sub-Commission on the Promotion and Protection of Human Rights. UN Doc.E/CN.4/Sub.2/2000/33, Geneva: UN Economic and Social Council, 21 June 2000, paragraph 98-100.

[78] Gott, Richard, *Cuba: A New History.* New Haven and London: Yale University Press. 2004

b)- Legislative and Public Policy Framework

In 2013, the U N passed a resolution condemning the embargo for the 22nd consecutive year. The vote was 188/2, only Israel supported the US policy. On the same token, President Obama's new policy suggests the overall U.S. embargo on trade with Cuba remains in place and can only be lifted by Congressional action.

In fact, my opinion is mostly based by taking into account the legislative and public policy framework, the implication of international law, or human rights and humanitarian law, and after establishing the international and national standards of embargo, and the regulations. Standards whereas the United Nations give the right to impose sanctions, Article 39 of the Charter gives the right to take sanctions; however these sanctions are to maintain or restore international peace and security if there exists a threat to or breach of peace or an act of aggression.

Article 1 paragraph 1 specifies that the threat must not be determined on the basis of ulterior political motives and must be genuine international concern; the sanctions must not be unjust or that they do not in any way violate any principle of international law, as the Charter outlaws ineffective or unjust sanctions or those that violate norms of international law.[79]

Further, Article 1 paragraph 3 of the Charter requires that issues of pressing humanitarian nature be solved and not to cause them, and that the sanctions must not result undue hardships for the people, and that sanctions that directly or indirectly cause deaths would be a violation of the right to life,

---

[79] United Nations Charter, Chapter VII, Article 39. http://www.un.org/en/sections/un-charter/chapter-vii/index.html

right to security of the person, health, etc... Thus, the Charter is against sanctions that lower economic standards and that create health problems.[80]

On the other hand, the Universal Declaration of Human Rights endorses the right to live in its Article 3, the right to an adequate standard of living, to food, clothing housing and medical care, in its Articles 5 and 25. On the same token, the International Covenants on Human Rights reiterate the rights to an adequate standard of living as well and the right to health in their Articles 11 and 12, and the right life in Article 6. In addition, The Hague Convention and Regulations goes further in its Article 50 and provides that no general penalty, financial or otherwise shall be imposed upon the population.[81]

The Geneva Conventions of 1949 go beyond and mandate the free passage of medical provisions in Convention IV, Protocol I, Article 54 requires the protection of objects indispensable to the survival of the civilian population, while article 70 provides for relief actions for the benefit of the civilian population, and Article 14 of Protocol II provides for the protection of objects indispensable to the survival of the civilian population.[82] Moreover, the General Assembly's resolutions relation to the protection of persons during conflicts provide that women and children belonging to the civilian population and finding themselves in circumstances of emergency shall not be deprived of shelter, food, medical aid or other inalienable rights.[83]

---

[80] United Nations Charter, Chapter VII, Article1, para. 3.. http://www.un.org/en/sections/un-charter/chapter-vii/index.html

[81] International Committee Of The Red Cross https://www.icrc.org/en

[82] The Geneva Conventions of 1949 and their Additional Protocols https://www.icrc.org/eng/war-and-law/treaties-customary-law/geneva-conventions/overview-geneva-conventions.htm

[83] General Assembly Resolutions, http://www.un.org/en/sections/documents/general-assembly-resolutions/index.html

In addition to all of the above, using U.N. Analyst Marc Bossuyt's six-prong test to evaluate the sanctions put on Cuba by the United States, to find out: first, if the sanctions are imposed for valid reasons; second, if the sanctions target the proper parties; third, if the sanctions target the proper goods and objects; fourth, if the sanctions are reasonably time-limited; fifth, if the sanctions are effective; sixth, if the sanctions are free from protest arising from violations of the principles of humanity and of the dictates of the public conscience. The answer to these questions relating the issue on the US/Cuba sanctions will demonstrate that the US has failed Bossuyt's test.[84]

The US government have used its power and authority and acted contrary to the Charter of the United Nations by restricting the direct import of medicine and medical equipment and supplies, and by imposing those restrictions on companies operating in third countries. Today, the US President is finally meeting the mind of the UN General Assembly, the Inter-American Commission on Human Rights, Amnesty International, and decides what it should have done a long time ago, to lift the embargo.

c)- Laws

Many laws have been enacted that are subject to the Cuban embargo. Some of them were against Cuba while some were supposed to be in the advantage of Cuba:

The Trading with the Enemy Act of 1917 (TWEA) grants the authority to the President of the USA to force economic sanctions against foreign nations by prohibiting, limiting or regulating

---

[84] Bossuyt, Marc. Em. Prof. THE ADVERSE CONSEQUENCES OF ECONOMIC SANCTIONS ON THE ENJOYMENT OF HUMAN RIGHTS

trade and financial transactions with hostile countries in times of war. In 1933, the US Congress amended section 5(b) of the Act, giving the President authority to impose comprehensive embargoes against foreign countries during "the time of war or during any other period of national emergency declared by the President". Based on the provision of "national emergency", President Dwight D. Eisenhower suspended trade with Cuba, a few days after his administration broke diplomatic relations with the country on 3 January 1961.[85]

The TWEA prohibits any type of trade or financial transaction, including those related to travel, transportation or business, in times of war or when a national emergency has been declared in relation to a specific country. In practice, these prohibitions force a ban on among other things, travel to and from Cuba, commerce and remittances.[86]

In 1977, Congress one more time amended the TWEA by limiting the President's powers to impose sanctions the Act provides for during time of war only.[87] However, Congress permitted the temporary continuation of presidential authority to maintain economic sanctions on countries as a result of a "national emergency" affirmed by the President before 1 July 1977. In addition, the President may "extend the exercise of such authorities for one-year periods upon a determination for each such extension that the exercise of such authorities

---

[85] Trading With the Enemy Act of 1917. US Code, Title 50, Appendix – War and National Defense, (ACT OCT. 6, 1917, CH. 106, 40 STAT. 411). Available at: http://uscode.house.gov/pdf/2001/2001usc50a.pdf

[86] Trading With the Enemy Act of 1917. US Code, Title 50, Appendix – War and National Defense, (ACT OCT. 6, 1917, CH. 106, 40 STAT. 411). Available at: http://uscode.house.gov/pdf/2001/2001usc50a.pdf

[87] Trading With the Enemy Act of 1917. US Code, Title 50, Appendix – War and National Defense, (ACT OCT. 6, 1917, CH. 106, 40 STAT. 411).

with respect to such country for another year is in the national interest of the United States."[88]

Since 1978, all US presidents gave out memorandums or presidential determinations extending under the TWEA, for one year at a time, the situation of "national emergency" with respect to Cuba on the grounds that it is "in the national interest of the United States".[89] In September 2008, President George W. Bush delivered a determination "continuing for 1 year, until September 14, 2009, the exercise of those authorities with respect to Cuba as implemented by the Cuban Assets Control Regulations, 31 C.F.R. Part 515."[90]

Cuba is the only country that confronts economic and trade sanctions from the USA under the provisions of the TWEA. In September 2009, President Barack Obama faces the option of issuing a determination that would continue the "national emergency" for another year under the TWEA with respect to Cuba or simply letting it expire.[91]

---

[88] Trading With the Enemy Act of 1917. US Code, Title 50, Appendix – War and National Defense, (ACT OCT. 6, 1917, CH. 106, 40 STAT. 411).

[89] Presidential Determination No. 2008–27 of September 12, 2008, Federal Register Vol. 73, No. 181, September 17, 2008. "Continuation of the Exercise of Certain Authorities Under the Trading With the Enemy Act". Available at: http://frwebgate2.access.gpo.gov/cgibin/
TEXTgate.cgi?WAISdocID=R4hn0F/0/1/0&WAISaction=retrieve.

[90] Presidential Determination No. 2008–27 of September 12, 2008, Federal Register Vol. 73, No. 181, September 17, 2008. "Continuation of the Exercise of Certain Authorities Under the Trading With the Enemy Act".

[91] In June 2008, President George W. Bush terminated his authority under the TWEA with regards to North Korea. See Presidential Proclamation 8271—Termination of the Exercise of Authorities Under the Trading With the Enemy Act With Respect to North Korea, available at:
http://frwebgate2.access.gpo.gov/cgibin/TEXTgate.cgi?WAISdocID=R4hn0F/1/1/0&WAISaction=retrieve.

In 1961, the US Congress approved the Foreign Assistance Act, Section 620A, which forbids any assistance to all communist countries, and to any other country which gave assistance to Cuba. It also authorizes the US President to "establish and maintain a total embargo upon all trade between the United States and Cuba".[92]

On 3 February 1962, acting under the authority of the Foreign Assistance Act, President John F. Kennedy suspended all trade with Cuba. He imposed, by Presidential Proclamation 3447, an embargo on all trade with Cuba, prohibiting the "importation into the United States of all goods of Cuban origin and goods imported from or through Cuba" and "all exports from the United States to Cuba". President Kennedy led the Secretary of the Treasury to implement the prohibition of all imports from Cuba and the Secretary of Commerce to impose the embargo on all exports to Cuba. The proclamation does not contain time limits or conditions for the lifting of the embargo and is still in effect, although since then the embargo has been written into law and expanded by regulations and new legislation.[93]

In 1963, the US government issued the Cuban Assets Controls Regulations (CACR) under section 5(b) of the Trading With the Enemy Act of 1917. The stated goal of the sanctions is to "isolate the Cuban government economically and deprive it of U.S. dollars."[94] The sanctions froze all Cuban assets in the

---

[92] Foreign Assistance Act of 1961, Sec. 620

[93] Presidential Proclamation 3447, Embargo on All Trade With Cuba, 3 February 1962. Available at John T. Woolley and Gerhard Peters, The American Presidency Project [online]. Santa Barbara, CA: University of California (hosted), Gerhard Peters (database), http://www.presidency. ucsb.edu/ws/?pid=58824; US International Trade Commission, The Economic Impact of US Sanctions With Respect to Cuba, 2001 pages 2-4.

[94] US Department of the Treasury, Office of Foreign Assets Control, What you need to know about the US embargo. An overview of the Cuban

USA and mandated the US Treasury Department to regulate all commercial transactions with Cuba, including authorized travel to Cuba by US nationals.[95] Although the regulations do not ban travel itself, freedom of movement between the USA and Cuba has been limited because all transactions related to travel to Cuba are restricted. These include food, hotel accommodation, transportation, items for personal use by travelers, and the sale of aero plane tickets in the USA. The CACR has been modified over the last four decades; travel restrictions were eased under the presidency of Jimmy Carter and then tightened again under the presidency of George W. Bush.[96]

Furthermore, the CACR prohibited the direct or indirect export of US products, services and technology to Cuba. The Treasury's Department Office of Foreign Assets Control still remains in charge of interpreting and implementing the provisions of the embargo through a set of regulations. The CACR also provides for criminal penalties for violation of the sanctions, ranging up to 10 years in prison, corporate fines of up to US$1 million and individual fines of up to US$250,000. Civil penalties of up to US$55,000 can also be imposed.[97]

Assets Control Regulations, Title 31 Part 515 of the US Code of Federal Regulations, in http://www.treas.gov/offices/enforcement/ofac/programs/cuba/cuba.pdf

[95] US Department of the Treasury, Office of Foreign Assets Control, What you need to know about the US embargo. An overview of the Cuban Assets Control Regulations, Title 31 Part 515 of the US Code of Federal Regulations, in http://www.treas.gov/offices/enforcement/ofac/programs/cuba/cuba.pdf

[96] US Department of the Treasury, Office of Foreign Assets Control, What you need to know about the US embargo. An overview of the Cuban Assets Control Regulations, Title 31 Part 515 of the US Code of Federal Regulations, in http://www.treas.gov/offices/enforcement/ofac/programs/cuba/cuba.pdf

[97] US Department of the Treasury, Office of Foreign Assets Control, What you need to know about the US embargo. An overview of the Cuban Assets

In 1992, President Bush signed the Cuban Democracy Act (the Torricelli Act) into law, forbidding subsidiaries of US companies from trading with Cuba, US nationals from travelling to Cuba and remittances being sent to the country. One of the stated goals of the Cuban Democracy Act (CDA) was to "seek a peaceful transition to democracy and a resumption of economic growth in Cuba through the careful application of sanctions directed at the Castro government and support for the Cuban people".[98]

The CDA seeks to "encourage the governments of other countries that conduct trade with Cuba to restrict their trade and credit relations."[99] It also tries to limit international cooperation towards Cuba by imposing "sanctions on any country that provides assistance to Cuba", including ending US assistance for those countries and by disqualifying them from benefiting from any program of reduction or forgiveness of debt owed to the USA.

The CDA states that exports of medicines and medical supplies, equipment and instruments shall not be restricted. Yet, these products may be exported to Cuba, from the USA or US subsidiaries based in another country "only if the President determines that the United States Government is able to verify, by onsite inspections and other appropriate means, that the exported item is to be used for the purposes for which it was

---

Control Regulations, Title 31 Part 515 of the US Code of Federal Regulations. For a list of penalties imposed to individuals and companies travelling to or doing business with Cuba see: OFAC Civil Penalties Enforcement Information, available at: http://www.treas.gov/offices/enforcement/ofac/civpen/.

[98] US Department of the Treasury, Cuban Democracy Act (CDA), United States Code, Title 22, Foreign Regulations and Intercourse, Chapter 69, http://www.treas.gov/offices/enforcement/ofac/legal/statutes/cda.pdf

[99] Cuba Democracy Act, section 6003.

intended and only for the use and benefit of the Cuban people."[100] This requirement does not apply to donations of medicines for humanitarian purposes to NGOs in Cuba. However, by imposing on-site verifications, the CDA makes the export of medicines and medical supplies to Cuba virtually impossible.

According to the US Department of Commerce, "under the CDA, the on-site monitoring requirement applies to all sales, and also applies to all donations of medical equipment, instruments and supplies. Monitoring also applies to donations of medicines except to nongovernmental organizations for humanitarian purposes."[101] In addition, a special license must be obtained from the US government prior to the export of any of these goods and "export license applications for most goods are subject to a policy of denial, although some specific goods are subject to case-by-case review".[102] The government of the USA was certainly not able to carry out the on-site inspections and therefore the burden fell on the exporters, making them

---

[100] Section 6004 of the Cuba Democracy Act [(CDA), 22 USC Sec. 6004] provides:

"Sec. 6004. Support for Cuban people (a) Provisions of law affected The provisions of this section apply notwithstanding any other provision of law, including section 2370(a) of this title, and notwithstanding the exercise of authorities, before October 23, 1992, under section 5(b) of the Trading With the Enemy Act [12 U.S.C. 95a, 50 U.S.C. App. 5(b)], the International Emergency Economic Powers Act [50 U.S.C. 1701 et seq.], or the Export Administration Act of 1979 [50 U.S.C. App. 2401 et seq.].

http://uscode.house.gov/download/pls/22C69.txt

[101] Section 6004 of the Cuba Democracy Act [(CDA), 22 USC Sec. 6004] provides:

"Sec. 6004. Support for Cuban people

http://uscode.house.gov/download/pls/22C69.txt

[102] Bureau of Industry and Security, US Department of Commerce, Guidelines on Sales and

Donations of Medicines and Medical Equipment to Cuba.

http://www.bis.doc.gov/policiesandregulations/medsht.htm.

subject to severe sanctions as included in the CACR if the procedures were not followed.

The tightening of the embargo through the CDA provides for humanitarian assistance by allowing the donation from individuals or US NGOs of medicines to Cuban NGOs only for humanitarian purposes. yet, the CDA places conditions that food, medicine and medical supplies for humanitarian purposes can only be made available to Cuba when the government of Cuba has changed through free and fair elections.[103] The CDA made it impossible for foreign subsidiaries of US companies to trade with Cuba. Other provisions of the CDA include a 180-day prohibition from loading or unloading in US territory of any vessel that had entered Cuba to trade goods or services. In an attempt to restrict the government of Cuba from gaining access to US currency, the CDA limited remittances to Cuba only to finance the travel of Cubans to the USA.

In 1996, the US Congress approved new legislation aiming at strengthening the enforcement of the US embargo against Cuba. In March 1996, President Bill Clinton signed into law the Cuban Liberty and Democratic Solidarity (Libertad) Act, most commonly known as the Helms Burton Act. This act further wrote into law the sanctions against Cuba. In particular, it sought to "strengthen international sanctions against the Castro government", and to "plan for support of a transition government leading to a democratically elected government in Cuba."[104]

---

[103] Bureau of Industry and Security, US Department of Commerce, Guidelines on Sales and Donations of Medicines and Medical Equipment to Cuba.

[104] Section 6006 of the Cuba Democracy Act (CDA), 22 USC Sec. 6006, Policy toward a transitional Cuban Government http://uscode.house.gov/download/pls/22C69.txt,

The Helms-Burton Act is divided into four titles. Title I: "Strengthening international sanctions against the Castro government" aims, among other things, at cutting Cuba's economic assistance and trading relationships with third countries, and opposing Cuba's membership in international financial institutions by instructing US executive directors in each institution to oppose the admission of Cuba as a member.

In fact, Cuba is barred from membership of the International Monetary Fund, the International Bank for Reconstruction and Development, the International Development Association, the International Finance Corporation, the Multilateral Investment Guarantee Agency and the Inter-American Development Bank.[105] Any loan or assistance provided by any of these institutions to the government of Cuba will result in the custody of the same amount by the US Secretary of Treasury from payment to that institution.

Title I also reaffirms the provisions of the CDA, in particular its extra-territorial aspects, including the imposition of penalties on foreign companies doing business in Cuba.

Title II of the Act: "Assistance to a free and independent Cuba" establishes the steps for the "termination of the US embargo against Cuba". These include a presidential determination, in consultation with Congress, suspending certain provisions of law such as section 620(a) of the Foreign Assistance Act of 1961, the Cuban Democracy Act of 1992, and the regulations prohibiting transactions with Cuba. Other provisions of the law defining the US embargo can be suspended once a democratically elected government is in place in Cuba. Sections 205 and 206 of this title provide the requirements for

---

[105] Cuba Liberty and Democratic Solidarity (Libertad) Act of 1996, One Hundred Fourth Congress of the United States of America.

determining a Cuban transition government and a democratic government. One of those requirements is the return to US nationals of property nationalized by the Cuban government after 1 January 1959.

This title also defines what US policy would be "towards a transition government and a democratically elected government". Under the title's provisions, the US government will provide its assistance-economic, food, medicine, medical supplies and equipment-to a transition government in Cuba and to the people of Cuba. It will also encourage other countries to do the same. Furthermore, Title II, section 202(iii) states: "only after a transition government in Cuba is in power, freedom of individuals to travel to visit their relatives without any restrictions shall be permitted".

Title III of the Helms-Burton Act: "Protection of property rights of United States Nationals" provides for compensation and allows US nationals to sue foreign companies deemed to have gained from investments in property (the Act uses the term "traffic in property") that belonged to US nationals prior to its nationalization by the Cuban government. This provision is allegedly aimed at preventing foreign investment in Cuba. The enforcement of Title III has been suspended since the Helms-Burton Act was approved by Congress. President Bill Clinton first suspended for six months the possibility of launching legal actions against foreign companies. Since then, US presidents, including Barack Obama, have issued a waiver postponing the enforcement of Title III for six months at a time.

Title IV: "Exclusion of certain aliens" provides for the exclusion or expulsion from the USA of those who "traffic in confiscated property", including executives and employees-and their family members-from foreign companies that invest in

Cuba in properties that belonged to US nationals before their nationalization by the Cuban government.

In October 2000 the US Congress passed the Trade Sanctions Reform and Export Enhancement Act (TSRA), which started to relax the enforcement of the economic and trade embargo and allowed the sale of agricultural goods and medicine to Cuba for humanitarian reasons. Since 2002, the USA has been the major supplier of food and agricultural products to Cuba. From 2005, US regulations required these exports to be on a cash-in-advance basis with full payment before the products were shipped to Cuba, and the transactions had to be made through banks in a third country. In 2008, Cuba imported more than US$700 million worth of food and agricultural products from the USA. In March 2009, the US government eased these restrictions, allowing Cuba to continue buying food and agricultural products and pay after shipment.[106]

Under the TSRA, exports of food and agricultural products to Cuba remain regulated by the Department of Commerce and require a license for export or re-export. The export of medicines and medical supplies continues to be severely limited. Although the TSRA considers the export of medicine, this legislation does not replace the Cuban Democracy Act of 1992 and therefore the necessity of a presidential certificate through onsite verifications remains in force.[107]

Over the past few years, Democrat and Republican members of Congress have introduced several bills to the US Senate

---

[106] US Department of the Treasury. Trade Sanctions Reform and Export Enhancement Act of 2000 (TSRA) Programhttps://www.treasury.gov/resource-center/sanctions/Programs/Pages/tsra.aspx
[107] US Department of the Treasury. Trade Sanctions Reform and Export Enhancement Act of 2000 (TSRA) Programhttps://www.treasury.gov/resource-center/sanctions/Programs/Pages/tsra.aspx

and House of Representatives aimed at easing or lifting the embargo. No action has been taken on any of them in Congress and some did not pass examination by different committees at the House or Representatives or the Senate. Hostility to the US embargo continues to grow as many see financial opportunities for trading with Cuba. The agro-industry successfully lobbied the US Congress to ease restrictions on the export of their products to Cuba with the adoption of the TSRA. On the first session of the 111th Congress, convened on 6 January 2009, there are now five bills promoting greater commercial and trade openness towards Cuba.

The office of the Resident Co-coordinator of the United Nations system for operational activities for development points out that "The negative impact of the embargo is pervasive in the social, economic and environmental dimensions of human development in Cuba, severely affecting the most vulnerable socioeconomic groups of the Cuban population."[108]

International law, including human rights law, provides limits to the imposition of sanctions.[109] There is growing recognition that in imposing sanctions, such as trade embargoes, states must take into account the effects that these sanctions may have on the enjoyment of economic, social and cultural rights in the country affected, must effectively monitor its consequences on the realization of these rights and take steps to address any adverse impact on the population of the affected state.

---

[108] Necessity of ending the economic, commercial and financial embargo imposed by the United States of America against Cuba, Report of the Secretary-General, A/63/93, 1 August 2008, p. 83.

[109] For an analysis of these limitations, see "The adverse consequences of economic sanctions on the enjoyment of human rights", a working paper submitted by Marc Bossuyt to the Sub Commission on the Promotion and Protection of Human Rights, E/CN.4/Sub.2/2000/33.

This recognition stems directly from the obligation of states under the UN Charter to promote human rights.[110] It is also derived from Article 2 of the International Covenant on Economic, Social and Cultural Rights (ICESCR), which requires states parties to "take steps, individually and through international assistance and co-operation, especially economic and technical, to the maximum of its available resources, with a view to achieving progressively the full realization of the rights recognized in the present Covenant..." In this report, Amnesty International focuses on the impact of the US embargo on the right to health.[111]

The USA signed, in October 1977, but has not yet ratified the ICESCR. As such, while not legally bound by its provisions, it is obliged to not defeat the purpose of the Covenant. According to article 18 of the 1969 Vienna Convention on the Law of Treaties, signed on 24 April 1970 by the USA, "a State is obliged to refrain from acts which would defeat the object and purpose of a treaty when: (a) it has signed the treaty or has exchanged instruments constituting the treaty subject to ratification, acceptance or approval, until it shall have made its intention clear not to become a party to the treaty." [112]

The Committee on Economic, Social and Cultural Rights has noted that the obligation of states to protect "at least the core content of the economic, social and cultural rights" of the affected people in the state targeted by sanctions derives from the Charter of the United Nations to promote respect for

[110] Articles 1, 55 and 56 of the UN Charter.
[111] Necessity of ending the economic, commercial and financial embargo imposed by the United States of America against Cuba, Report of the Secretary-General, A/63/93, 1 August 2008,
[112] Necessity of ending the economic, commercial and financial embargo imposed by the United States of America against Cuba, Report of the Secretary-General, A/63/93, 1 August 2008,

all human rights.[113] For the past 14 years, the UN Secretary-General has documented the negative impact of the US embargo on Cuba.

On May 29, 2015, the US removed Cuba from the list of state sponsors of terrorism.[114] Furthermore, on July 1, 2015, diplomatic relations have been formally reestablished with Cuba and to reopen embassies.[115]

On July 20, 2015, as a sign of renewed diplomatic relations, the Cuban flag was raised over Washington DC embassy for the first time after 54 years.[116] And shortly after, US Secretary of State John Kerry traveled to Cuba to hoist the American flag over the US embassy there.[117]

IV- Future trends

a)- What the US seems to be going to decide

The United States has taken steps to ease travel and remittance restrictions, release Cuban spies, and re-open each

---

[113] General Comment No. 8 of the Committee on Economic, Social and Cultural Rights, The relationship between economic sanctions and respect for economic, social and cultural rights, particularly paragraphs 7 and 8.

[114] The Wall Street Journal: Cuba Officially Removed From U.S. State Sponsor of Terrorism List. http://www.wsj.com/articles/cuba-officially-removed-from-u-s-state-sponsor-of-terrorism-list-1432913160

[115] Pestano, Andrew V. World News: United States and Cuba formally reestablish diplomatic relations; to open embassies. July 1, 2015 at 11:29 AM

[116] ITV Report: US flag raised over embassy in Cuba for the first time in 54 years. 14 August 2015 at 3:45pm http://www.itv.com/news/2015-08-14/us-flag-raised-over-embassy-in-cuba-for-the-first-time-in-54-years/

[117] ABC News: US secretary of state John Kerry raises flag at US embassy in Havana on historic trip; calls for 'genuine democracy' in Cuba. Updated 14 Aug 2015, 3:38pm http://www.abc.net.au/news/2015-08-15/us-sec-of-state-john-kerry-arrives-in-cuba-on-historic-trip/6699530

other's embassies. Cuba on its side, agreed to release 53 Cubans identified by the United States as political prisoners, as well as an American and an unnamed intelligence agent who had been imprisoned for nearly 20 years.[118]

Today President Obama is renewing calls to end the Cuban embargo. He is taking more executive actions to increase the changes. The US senators urged President Obama to loosen travel restrictions further so that Americans can conduct independent cultural exchanges in Cuba rather than go with tour groups as U.S. regulations currently require. In addition, Obama authorized new exports as part of the policy shift, including tools and equipment for Cuba's small private sector. The U.S. and Cuba are close to completing civil aviation talks, which will make it very much easier for travelers to go to Cuba from the U.S.[119]

b)- What could be the reason(s) or motive(s)

Before projecting, we need to find out what could be the reasons or motives for this whole scenario – President Obama urges Congress to take steps to lift Cuba embargo. why? why now? The true reasons seem to be unclear, just like it was unclear why they wanted Cuba so bad.

It could be since the US tried to intervene so many times into Cuba, none of them has worked; now they want to do the opposite to see if it might work.

---

[118] Holmes, Kristen. Obama 'very much' wants to go to Cuba Updated 12:57 PM ET, Mon December 14, 2015 http://www.cnn.com/2015/12/14/politics/ obama-cuba-trip-yahoo-news/index.html
[119] Holmes, Kristen. Obama 'very much' wants to go to Cuba Updated 12:57 PM ET, Mon December 14, 2015 http://www.cnn.com/2015/12/14/politics/ obama-cuba-trip-yahoo-news/index.html

It could be that they are using Sun Tzu's principle in his book The Art of War. The Art of War is an ancient Chinese military dissertation or essay attributed to Sun Tzu, a high-ranking military general, a strategist, a tactician, and a member of the 'Realpolitik' of his time.[120] The whole text is devoted to warfare; it is thought of as an ultimate work on military strategy and tactics. It contains the most famous and influential of China's Seven Military Classics and remained the most important military treatise in Asia for the last two thousand years. It had influenced Eastern and Western military thinking, business tactics, legal strategy and beyond.[121]

The book has been translated in French, and partially into English.[122] Diverse leaders from all over the world have drawn inspiration from it. It has been the subject of law books and legal articles on the trial process, including negotiation tactics and trial strategy. Its doctrine or philosophy has been applied to many fields outside of the military, also in the world of sports, and electronic sports.[123] It sounds like a New Haven School whereas its doctrine can be applied anytime anywhere in any situation when trying to find a solution.

The Art of War is much about how to fight wars without in reality having to battle. The Art of War gives tips on how to overcome one's opponent so that physical battle is not necessary. In fact, it has found application as a training guide for many competitive endeavors that do not involve actual

---

[120] Wealth and Power

[121] Sawyer, Rd. Ralph. The Seven Military Classics of Ancient China. New York: Basic Books. 2007. p. 149.

[122] Giles, Lionel. The Art of War by Sun Tzu-Special Edition. Special Edition Books. 2007. p. 62.

[123] Barnhizer, David. The Warrior Lawyer: Powerful Strategies for Winning Legal Battles Irvington-on-Hudson, NY: Bridge Street Books, 1997.

combat. Several Japanese companies and others make the book required reading for their key executives.[124]

Most importantly, the Department of the Army in the United States, through its Command and General Staff College, lists The Art of War as one example of a book that may be kept at a military unit's library.[125] The Art of War is listed on the Marine Corps Professional Reading Program known as the Commandant's Reading List, and it is recommended reading for all United States Military intelligence personnel and is required reading for all CIA officers.[126]

Even the Russian Komitet gosudarstvennoy bezopasnosti *(KGB)* have widely used some strategies in the Art of War.[127]

c) Possible Projection or Prediction

Bearing in mind what could be its motives, it is probable that the US this time may be using Sun Tzu's tactics to finally win this cold war against Cuba. For I find it a bit awkward that after all these years of fight, they come and do this quick and easy switch. They may have in mind to apply the doctrine of "je t'embrasse pour mieux t'ettouffer," a French phrase that literally translates I kiss you, or rather I embrace you to better struggle you, in other words, I keep you closer to me so I can easier catch you.

---

[124] Jeffrey, D (2010). "A Teacher Diary Study to Apply Ancient Art of War Strategies to Professional Development". The International Journal of Learning 7 (3): 21–36.
[125] Army, U. S. (1985). Military History and Professional Development. U. S. Army Command and General Staff College, Fort Leavenworth, Kansas: Combat Studies Institute. 85-CSI-21 85.
[126] Marine Corps Professional Reading Program
[127] Yevgenia Albats and Catherine A. Fitzpatrick. The State Within a State: The KGB and Its Hold on Russia—Past, Present, and Future. 1994. ISBN 0-37452738-5, chapter Who was behind perestroika?

It could be that the US want to be part of what Cuba has accomplished, the best doctors, the cigars, the culture, or may be Castro's clever philosophy, or they want to apply the doctrine of why don't we all get along and share?

A White House official said, the restitution of diplomatic relationship is being done because they believe that the policy of the past has not worked and ... the best way to bring democracy and prosperity to Cuba is through a different kind of policy."

However, regardless of what could be the reasons, the embargo should be released. It will tremendously benefit both countries culturally, economically, and more.

V- Alternatives and Recommendations in the Global Common Interest

Marc Bossuyt, a member of the Permanent Court of Arbitration in The Hague and a former judge at the Belgian Constitutional Court, prepared a study for the Sub-Commission on the promotion and Protection of Human Rights, called 'The adverse consequences of economic sanctions on the enjoyment of human Rights,' stated that the US embargo violates human rights law in two distinct ways.

Firstly, "the fact that the United States is the major regional economic power and the main source of new medicines and technologies means that Cuba is subject to deprivations that impinge on its citizens' human rights." Secondly, by passing legislation that "tries to force third-party countries into embargoing Cuba as well" – the 1992 Torricelli Act – the US government attempted to turn "a unilateral embargo into a multilateral embargo through coercive measures, the only effect of which will be to deepen further the suffering of the Cuban people and increase the violation of their human rights".[128]

The theory behind economic sanctions is that economic pressure on a country including on its civilians will translate into pressure on the government for change. But this kind of theory shows evidence of inefficacy as these sanctions are used as a coercive tool as the impact of the suffering of civilians overbalance the projected desired political effects. These sanctions sometimes tend to worsen civilian hardship and give more political advantages to the elites and the ruling group. The sanctions make the poor become poorer, and the rich richer as they can take control over smuggling and the black market.[129]

On the hand, these sanctions are designed to affect the political leaders or those responsible for the breach of peace while leaving the innocent civilian population alone. These sanctions tend to eliminate civilian suffering while putting significant pressure on the government itself and bringing compliance with human rights and humanitarian law and increasing their chances of success. These sanctions also target the personal foreign assets access to foreign financial markets of members of the government, the ruling elites, and the members of the military.

It is in light of the above details that I can suggest that The

---

[128] Bossuyt, Marc: The Adverse Consequences of Economic Sanctions on the Enjoyment of Human Rights, Working Paper prepared for the Commission On Human Rights, Sub-Commission on the Promotion and Protection of Human Rights. UN Doc.E/CN.4/Sub.2/2000/33, Geneva: UN Economic and Social Council, 21 June 2000, paragraph 98-100.

[129] The Bossuyt Report: Economic and Social Council: The Adverse Consequences of Economic Sanctions E/CN.4/Sub.2/2000/33, June 21, 2000 https://www.globalpolicy.org/global-taxes/42501-the-adverse-consequences-of-economic-sanctions.html#30

United States could have instead used 'Smart sanctions' to deal with the Castro regime as an alternative.

However, as a recommendation, while the embargo should be released, because today "it's the right thing to do," as President Obama puts it.[130] America should be open-minded to ALL kinds of government, and stop thinking that only his is best. Other options sometimes may culturally fit other places better.

The US should also now accept the fact that embargo is not a solution to win access to other countries. Embargo, if not being used to protect people from 'genocide' or from 'ethnic cleansing,' it should not be lightly used against a whole country only because of one person's opinion or choice of government type. When a country already so poor, so underdeveloped, not being able to produce by itself, get sanctioned by a so powerful country, knowing that the sanctioning it, the country with its people will be destroyed because of it, embargo can be perceived as a crime against humanity. The United States knew that the Cuban people including children, and HIV/AIDS patients were dying of malnutrition, and or because of lack of medicines or medical supplies, in addition to the whole population who suffers of weakness, anemia because of lack of vitamins, they still suppressed the embargo and even made it worst at times.[131]

Embargo should be seen as a human right violation,

---

[130] Sean Piccoli, Cuba Scholar: 'Obama Thinks Raul Castro Is Going to Change?' Newmax, Dec. 27, 2014 http://www.newsmax.com/Newsmax-Tv/cuba-normalization-embargo-relations/2014/12/17/id/613600/

[131] Bossuyt, Marc: The Adverse Consequences of Economic Sanctions on the Enjoyment of Human Rights, Working Paper prepared for the Commission On Human Rights, Sub-Commission on the Promotion and Protection of Human Rights. UN Doc.E/CN.4/Sub.2/2000/33, Geneva: UN Economic and Social Council, 21 June 2000, paragraph 98-100.

it punishes people for their freedom of choice, cutting off relationships and closing economic doors with the idea that the people might starve to death. That is a crime; that is a violation of human right.

D- CONCLUSION

In sum, The U.S. International Trade Commission estimates American losses alone from the embargo as much as $1.2 billion annually. Ending the embargo would have obvious economic benefits for both Cubans and Americans. The US should release the embargo, put aside all differences and make peace with one another.

It should take, without further delay, the necessary steps towards lifting the economic, financial and trade embargo against Cuba, since the lifting of the embargo will require the US Congress to enact new legislation repealing the Cuban Democracy Act of 1992 and the Cuba Liberty and Solidarity (Libertad) Act of 1996. Amnesty International should now call on the US Congress, and pressure them in order for the lifting to be achieved within this current Congress session by adopting the bills already introduced in the House of Representatives and the Senate intended to that purpose.

"The Son is the image of the invisible God, the firstborn over all creation. For in him all things were created: things in heaven and on earth, visible and invisible, whether thrones or powers or rulers or authorities; all things have been created through him and for him. He is before all things, and in him all things hold together." (Colossians 1:15-17 NIV)

"He sits enthroned above the circle of the earth, and its people are like grasshoppers. He stretches out the heavens like a canopy, and spreads them out like a tent to live in. He brings princes to naught and reduces the rulers of this world to nothing. No sooner are they planted, no sooner are they sown, no sooner do they take root in the ground, than he blows on them and they wither, and a whirlwind sweeps them away like chaff." (Isaiah 40-22-24 NIV)

Out of all of the Bible verses on government, I come to the same conclusions:

God is the ultimate authority, as He has created all things and all of us. He is in control of the happenings of this world. What you see is not the end of the story...

OTHER REFERENCE

Wiessner, Siegfried, The New Haven School of Jurisprudence: A Universal Toolkit for Understanding and Shaping the Law (2010). Asia Pacific Law Review, Vol. 81, No. 1, p.45, 2010, St. Thomas University School of Law Research Paper No. 2, Available at SSRN: https://ssrn.com/abstract=2011130

Photo Reference

[1] http://epthinktank.eu/2015/02/25/change-in-us-cuba-relations/

Printed in the United States
by Baker & Taylor Publisher Services